WHEN GOD BECOMES REAL

WHEN GOD BECOMES REAL:
STORIES OF PRESENCE,
MODELS OF CHURCH

Bobbie McKay

Exploration Press

Chicago Theological Seminary

Chicago, Illinois

Library of Congress Cataloging-in-Publication Data

When God Becomes Real: stories of presence, models of church
by Bobbie McKay

Library of Congress Control Number (LCCN): 2007930623

Publisher:

Exploration Press
5757 S. University Avenue
Chicago, IL 60637-1507

ISBN: 978-0-9135-5271-1

Book design by Robert Barker/Barker Design

Printed in the U.S.A.

To my fabulous grandchildren,
who help me to see
that God is REAL;
and to Lew,
who shares every step of the journey!

Table of contents

INTRODUCTION

This book tells the story of a divine Love that meets human need in thousands of moments in which women and men experience the presence of God in their lives and are transformed. These "real life" encounters of God and the re-telling of such stories not only transform individuals but draw them into community, leading to new and quite unexpected models of church. In other words, when people find themselves in heart-to-heart, spirit-to-Spirit contact with God, they are also drawn into relationship with one another—and so become church, but not the sort of church that comes most quickly to mind. This church thrives without sanctuary, building or budgets, without priests, dogma or creed. It is a church of bridges, not walls. It begins simply, when a person becomes aware of God.

From birth, through the wonder of life and into the mystery of death, the Creative Center of the Universe, again and again, issues personal invitations of connection to each of us and then waits patiently for us to notice and respond. When we were children, we had a special *spiritual* awareness, which was a natural part of who we were. For a brief span of time, we could look at life spontaneously from the heart and soul of Spirit and experience life as a reflection of God everywhere. Unfortunately, that lens becomes blurred in the process of growth. We lose our uninhibited, open spirit as we make the "necessary" adjustments to life with its limits and controls. We become more self-conscious and learn to disregard our inner truths. We become ego-bound and reality-centered, choosing to weigh the plusses and minuses, the pro's and con's of life in a much more cautious manner. We let our awareness of God's invitation fade.

And, yet, sometimes, our connection to God's Spirit is reignited and we discover God once again in the midst of our lives, simply awaiting our return and our reunion. Whether this experience happens to an individual in ordinary life or to a group of people gathered as members of a religious or secular community, the outcome is always the same: *When God becomes real, transformation begins.*

Such stories are the foundation of this book.

Some encounters may take place where we worship. Others involve the painful recognition of the emptiness of our lives and the experience of the Living God where, and when, we least expected to find it. Some discover, in the sadness of loss and pain, the surprise of new life occurring in the midst of death and defeat. For most, it is a remembered story that reappears to bring us back into connection with God.

When God becomes *real* to us in any particular moment, we begin to understand the meaning of new life and transformation. We cannot see or touch God, nor can we make God do our bidding. But we can look for those experiences in which our plans have been interrupted or our goals suddenly redefined. In identifying those experiences, we discover the God of Surprise whose faithful and persistent agenda is always the same: *connection* and *transformation*. Sharing our stories of times when God was actively present in our lives creates a new and larger setting for reconciliation and healing in the world.

In the last fifty years, powerful changes in both society and in the family have made the presence of God seem remote or even non-existent for many. The most overt signs of these changes began in the 1960s when discordant and strident voices of young adults in our society rang out because they did not like what they saw happening in the world and were determined to let us know how they felt.

The crumbling of beliefs and institutions that we considered our "firm foundations" continued through each subsequent decade—continuing still in this new century—inundating us with such profound changes and crises in the family and in society that many came to feel lost in the resulting chaos. The world appeared to be on a fast and very different track from what was known and familiar. Whether we liked these differences or not, they appear to be "here to stay." Where can we find God in a world which seems so out of control, in a world where there seem to be no spiritual anchors?

Our churches were also challenged by these changes and experienced their own upheavals interwoven with the crises of the larger society. Even God's "house" was not exempt from the effects of change. Where, indeed, *was* God when long established and customary rules for life and living were being broken on every side?

The story this book will tell begins with those changes in society and the religious world that were catalytic in challenging the foundations and structures of our lives. It will continue with three models of community life that grew out of those wrenching yet transformative times—vivid examples of what can happen when God becomes real in the lives of individuals and groups, arenas in which our spirits and God's Spirit intersect and new life begins:

1. within a church setting (A Church in the Gym);
2. within an interfaith community outside of the religious establishment (A Church Without Walls); and,
3. within a large, international study of 150 interfaith congregations with ethnic, socioeconomic, geographic, preference and creedal diversity (A Church Beyond the Churches).

The book concludes with reflections and suggestions about ways in which God can become real in your life and your community—whether religious or secular.

In the interweaving of continuing change and the constancy of God's presence lies the opportunity to discover God's harmony and presence in this multi-dimensional world in which we live. As you witness the unfolding birth of each of these models, let them speak to your spirit and your heart. Then, let the reality of God's Presence guide you through the promise of transformation and into your own new life!

PART ONE

SEISMIC SHIFTS:
LOSING TOUCH WITH GOD

CHAPTER 1

UPHEAVALS:
UNRELENTING,
SOCIETY-WIDE CYCLES
OF CHANGE

*F*or nearly five decades, we've been inundated with the sound and fury of wave after wave of changes that have challenged the heart of our individual and family lives, tearing loose behavioral anchors and threatening to sink our religious institutions—at least in their familiar form.

We generally look back to the 1960s as the beginning of this new era of crisis and confrontation. Immediate explanations are easy to assume. The Vietnam War demanded the sacrifice of too many of our children and divided those of us who remained at home. The sexual revolution and the advent of the birth control pill obliterated the rules and restrictions surrounding sexual conduct. Long hair, psychedelic rock, and the increasing use of drugs and alcohol by our youth represented powerful symbols of a society that was changing its direction and would likely never return to the familiar hierarchy of "father knows best."

While historical turning points may seem easy to pin point, history has a way of living underground until conditions are ripe and ready for the arrival of change. In fact, there are likely to be forces and conditions already set in motion long before actual changes take place. We may have to look at the "history" of history if we are to understand and appreciate the power of these cycles of change. Nowhere is that more evident than in the events of the last fifty years in relation to profound changes in the family, society and the Church.

Change as a Course Correction

The eruptions of the 1960s serve as a "short-hand" picture of an irreversible shift in the direction of U.S. culture. In reality, these were simply a part of a larger and long overdue "course correction" that had been put in motion many years before. If we had been able to see the bigger picture (the "history" behind this history), we might have identified a new *cycle of change* that actually began right after World War I.

For a brief time, in the post-war years of the 1920s, there was relief and hope for peace, grounded in the conviction that WWI was the war to end all wars. Peace, prosperity and "good times" were "here to stay." But we were dead wrong. World War I was followed by the Great Depression, World War II, the Korean Conflict, and the Vietnam War.

With no time to deal with each of these major world events before the next one arrived, we were overdue for an explosion of reactive outrage for the inner pain and losses we had experienced for nearly half a century. That this rage would enter the world through the '60s generation who had not actually lived through some of these cataclysmic events took us by surprise. But we soon discovered they carried deep undercurrents within them that accumulate when human beings endure continuous and unrelenting pain. The residue of grief, loss and terror carried from one generation to the next finally overflowed its inner and hidden container as the Vietnam War wore on. It was simply too much for too long.

Changes in Society and Family

Families and other social institutions were staggered by this unexpected and sudden appearance of "in your face" adolescents and young adults, who expressed their strident discontent in language and actions that demanded our attention. Daily confrontations between the young and the not-so-young were being waged on new and uncomfortable battlegrounds.

As values and behavioral anchors shifted, resulting in more open aggression, the family began to break apart. New family forms appeared as the divorce rate increased, creating a fragile world of single parents and blended families. Pressured by adolescents "acting out" their fears and frustrations, parents found themselves losing confidence in their ability to cope as they plunged into new territories with few boundaries and little control.

A new "counter-culture" emerged and found its power outside the rules and regulations of the family and society. Many attracted to such marginal existences experimented with new kinds of relationships, while their drugs of choice provided them the means to ignore the messes they were creating. Hand in hand, the drug culture and its captives grew as suppliers and addicts found each other.

While the family and society seemed to be engaged in an unstoppable process of change, the Church—that solid, built-on-a-rock institution with God in charge, the place we turned to for strength, ethical guidance and moral substance—began to shift on its foundations as well.

Changes in the Church

These changes began quietly within the local church hierarchy as people began to question the authority of the church. Inevitably, quiet rumblings at the local level became amplified as they rose through denominational structures, combining and accumulating in the process.

The first issue involved the entrance of a growing number of women into seminary. Some of those who protested described women clergy as "usurping" the jobs of men and abandoning their families to pursue their own "selfish interests." Other opponents of women's ordination saw it as a simple question of historical precedent: "If Jesus had wanted women in his group of disciples, he would have chosen some. Since he didn't, it was clear he saw women as helpers, but not the genuine article!" A new kind of schism had come to life.

Later, women would shock and surprise the Church by insisting on a language of equality both in doctrine and worship. The strength of the resistance to changing the words to describe both God and humanity showed how powerful language is. Opening the conversation about women as ordained clergy and as shapers of the language of faith carried with it the potential for even more challenges in the very sanctuary of the Church.

Just how far these changes would go was anybody's guess. It was the season of change everywhere; no one was exempt and nowhere did solid ground appear to exist. The unavoidable processes of change had finally caught up with us and broken through the surface of our resistance and denial.

We were beginning to lose touch with the God we thought we knew.

Change Always Stirs the Waters of Resistance

We have a love-hate relationship with change. We seek change and we resist it. We work toward change and we fight against it. We want things to be better; but we don't want to have to change. In fact, change always provokes powerful forms of resistance, fostering new power struggles and divisions. But resistance to change is always our last—and least effective—method to prevent our world from collapsing.

When storms begin, they not only stir up waves, they also create a mix of sediment and debris that clouds and disturbs all the water and settles slowly, very slowly. The aftermath of the '60s, and the ongoing confusion that followed, created changes so drastic there simply was no way to go back to the way it was before.

Change as a rhythmic part of life pressures and moves our energy toward the future. It forces us to look at the reality that we cannot enter the future without leaving the past. It presents us with a point of no return, a kind of awe-filled "either-or" that we try to avoid at all costs. We want to keep it all just the same, thank you very much! Please don't *make* us change!

The Other Side of Change

But there is another side to cycles of change. They can also help us to break through states of complacency and stagnation and engage bottled-up forces of dissonance and resistance, pointing us toward a new harmony which was *unavailable* within the old structures and institutions. Since we cannot see into the future, we cannot know the *gifts* that change may also contain.

Experiences of profound change can be frightening and painful because the outcome is thoroughly obscured by our inability to see the *bigger* picture. In the midst of the chaos of change, we cry out: "Where in the world is God in all of this mess?" We wonder what we have done or not done to create these unholy upheavals. We seek to control the process by any possible means—to stop it, or at least to slow it down.

When one is living in the dark, the Light can seem distant or even non-existent. So it was for many of us in the late '60s and in the time since then. But in more rational moments, it was clear that these decades of change, throughout which we felt that the very center and heart of our lives and belief systems were collapsing, were part of a larger context which was steadily moving us *into the future*. The cause was not our failures or inadequacies and it certainly was not the absence of God. We came to see that there might be more going on in these chaotic cycles of change than we were seeing. Change can be a gift as well as a loss.

In fact, it is only when we finally understand that God is *always* discovered within the processes of change that we begin to recognize the gifts that can be ours, *if* we have the courage to enter into the process. Our societal and family upheavals were actually bringing us into the possibility of seeing God's presence in our lives in a *new way*. The future held promises waiting to be discovered.

God always *begins* when we realize our limitations and recognize the Mystery of God's generous and indescribable love in the midst of our lives. The process of change lies between those two realities.

Seeing them both is the heart of and key to the process.

8

CHAPTER 2

CHANGE ON THE MOVE:
RESTRUCTURING THE FAMILY,
GENERATION AFTER
GENERATION

The drumbeat of change was relentless. These changes were not just broad—effecting all aspects of life—but were also deep, reaching into our belief systems and self-understanding. The world changed so quickly that we began to see that children were not just different from their parents but were truly growing up in a very different world. Each succeeding generation after World War II received their own name to identify these changes.

While the peace and prosperity that followed World War II fooled many of us into thinking that all would become stable and calm, we could not have been more wrong. But we would not realize how wrong for some time. Like the post World War I era, good times appeared to be "here to stay" in 1945. The war had ended. Life was rich and full. Optimism prevailed! It was a time for the entrance of that special group of children, born between 1946 and 1964, and lovingly known as the Baby Boomers.

The Baby Boomers

Baby Boomers were the beloved children of the 1950s, living a postcard life of happy families and communities and well under our control and supervision. Churches were filled with children in Sunday School and confirmation class; teenagers did service projects to improve the community. Most seemed to follow the pattern of growing up, getting married, having children and then grandchildren. "Family" was central, important, valued. Contributing to family life and to one's community was a priority for most people. Our children were the children of a society that was eternally grateful to be finished with war.

Except that we weren't finished!

At the outer edges of our peaceful life, the Korean "conflict" had already begun in the late 1940s and early 1950s. The Vietnam war followed, catapulting the family out of any kind of "normalcy" or complacency. The brief interlude of peace was blanketed in the darkness of a new kind of war that would change all of our lives. The horrors of Vietnam would create a new breed of young people who broke open our denial systems and brought the visible reality of war into the very center of our families and communities.

The Flower Children

The 1960s emerged as the decade of the Flower Children, those adolescents and young adults whose very name reflected a deep, ironic outrage over this new wave of killing. They gathered in large groups and immediately gained our attention with their outrageous clothes; their harsh, electronic music; and, their aggressive demeanor, sexual openness and blatant drug use. Each new, provocative behavior contained an insistence that we hear their powerful "in your face" message against the war.

Paradoxically, while the huge public gatherings by which these "love children" (as they were sometimes called) sought our attention might be draped in the rhetoric of peace and love, they were filled with the strident sounds of contemporary music accompanied by the newest drugs and dealers.

Whatever their other motivations may have been, the Flower Children "took us on" to teach us that war was the wrong way to manage this brave new world. Their passive resistance to the killing was a highly effective strategy in raising our consciousness about the awful reality of war and the necessity to end it. But their protest was about more than the war. Relentlessly, they challenged our value systems, institutions, control and authority wherever and whenever they could. And we got the message.

Intermingled with the Flower Children of '60s emerged a new generation of young people following the Baby Boomers chronologically, but moving in very different directions.

Generation X

The Generation Xers (those children born between 1965 and 1981) were devastated by the onslaught of change in their critical, formative years. Disenfranchised by a society without anchors, they held on to each other and waited to see what the future would bring.

They were less passive-resistors to a war they couldn't tolerate then they were passive-reactors in their general approach to life. Reluctant to take actions which might require commitments, they chose to remain on the fringe of life rather than to jump into a future that was unknown and, therefore, potentially hazardous. For example, they preferred to live together rather than to marry. If they married, it was later than the previous generation. Decisions about having children were no longer automatic but were influenced by the state of the world and could be avoided indefinitely because of the availability of reliable birth control.

Having been born in the middle of the 1960s and 70s, living their early impressionable years through the Vietnam war and its aftermath of societal change, they bore the mark of that chaotic, transitional time in the essence of their being. Trust could backfire; promises could be broken; life was engulfed in change, with few reliable anchors.

Like the Flower Children, this generation also used drugs. But their drug of choice was "marijuana," a drug guaranteed to dull the mind and reduce one's passion and ability to succeed. They needed something to break the "free fall" of their early years and they found it in a new kind of passivity as an antidote to pain. Better to hold back than to leap into anything which required commitment or a willingness to change.

Unfortunately, prolonged passivity inhibits growth while nurturing anxiety and fear, making the future that much more terrifying. The longer one remains in that state, the harder it is to break out of it. Our Generation Xers were trapped in a no-win world without an exit strategy.

The Yuppies

The cycle of change shifted and moved in a new direction with the next generation. Enter the group of children born in the 1980s, better known as the Yuppies. Born to be "upwardly mobile," they were often described as more concerned about themselves, their successes and material goods than the needs or wishes of others. As a large and coveted group of consumers, their ability to purchase goods and services became their primary symbols of success.

These were the children of the Baby Boomers, and the products of a growing permissiveness in our society, which began in their early, formative years. It should have been no surprise that they became exactly what we had taught them to be.

Generation Y

Meanwhile, a small new group called Generation Y emerged. These children, born in a brief window between 1981 and 1995, arrived as a kind of antidote to the Generation Xers. Without carrying the same passivity or reaction-based behavior, they sought to live more conservatively, valuing a more measured lifestyle, without the excesses of previous generations. They were also living on the brink of a new century, as on a teeter-totter—balancing the old against the new. This ethos of transition permeated deeply into their lives. They provided us all with a glimpse of what was to come as the 20th century came to a close.

The Millennial (or, Y2K) Generation

Overlapping with Generation Y, the Millennial Generation arrived. These were children born between 1982 and 2003, their name indicating that those born in 1982 would likely graduate from high school in the year 2000. There numbers were impressive! This group "includes more children and youth in school than any other cohort in U.S. History."[1]

This Y2K group (as they were often called) had its own unique characteristics and were deeply affected by the impact of technology and the electronic world they occupied. In his book on American religion, George Gallup quotes a bullet-point description of Y2K kids by Wendy Murray Zoba:

- This generation's pulse runs fast. Bombarded by frequent images, they are in need of continual 'hits'.
- The TV/VCR remote control symbolizes their reality: change is constant; focus is fragmented.
- They've eaten from the tree of knowledge.
- They live for now.
- They are jaded. Nothing shocks them.
- They are a cyber-suckled community.
- They process concepts in narrative images (like Nike commercials).
- Their [bull] detectors are always on.
- They don't trust adults.[2]

Still, Gallup concludes: "In reaching out to them, we must not regard them as pathologies waiting to happen, but sparks of joy to be fanned aflame and nurtured."[3]

Conclusion

Between the birth of the first Baby Boomer in 1946 and the birth of the final Y2K kid in 2003, U.S. culture traversed a territory of deep and powerful changes. Society, community and the family took on constantly changing shapes. Change was clearly on the move! Six decades had produced six different kinds of life-styles, which involved the restructuring of both the family and community. Challenges to authority and control dominated the social landscape and one could scarcely recognize the world of 2003 from its roots in 1946.

As family and community structures gave way, the door opened to other societal issues that were not going to go away. Once the barriers of resistance and denial had been challenged, there was no more turning back from the reality of injustice and oppression in our society. Civil rights, real equality for women, gay/lesbian liberation, the end of poverty and disease were powerful arenas that demanded our attention. Yet, if one could see the larger picture, such struggles were also visible opportunities for reconciliation and healing in a world engulfed in change, and not simply expressions of rebellion.

Generally, cycles of change are most readily seen in retrospect. It was not until we reached the end of the 20th century that the full picture of this current cycle of change could begin to emerge in full Technicolor.

In the meantime, one institution became a critical "player" in the scenes of fear, frustration and uncertainty that inevitably arose during such a period of radical change in the structures of society. The church—which does not operate independently from society, the community and the family—tried valiantly to minister to any and all situations, to become more socially conscious, and to continue to be some manifestation of God's presence in the world. But the church was also engulfed in its own process of change and could no longer avoid the shockwave of declining membership and revenues. The church was now fully engaged in its own identity crisis.

CHAPTER 3

ECCLESIAL UPHEAVALS: CHALLENGES TO TRADITIONAL CHURCH STRUCTURES

*C*hallenges over authority and control taking place in the larger society were mirrored by similar struggles in the church. Conservatives and liberals argued over issues of racial justice, women clergy, inclusive language, and the ordination of homosexuals. Each of these controversies threatened to fracture congregations and denominations. But these struggles were also embedded in larger issues of identity and survival, which emerged as other forces threatened to put the traditional, mainstream church out of business.

The New Age Movement

The New Age movement arose in this country in the last few decades of the 20th century, offering new spiritual paths and alternative lifestyles to those seeking a religious life but one situated beyond the confines of institutional rules and mandates. The conservative religious world of the 1950s became a backdrop for newer and more exciting ideas and opportunities from different cultures and life styles. People could now be spiritual without ever having to enter a church.

In a world challenged by change and upheaval, these new spiritual paths offered opportunities for peace, serenity and healing. Our minds, bodies and spirits could be focused on a new "recipe" for religion and health. It was like living water for the thirsty and manna for the hungry. Being broadly inclusive, covering eastern as well as western thought and philosophy, the New Age movement offered a container for everyone!

The first step from the dominance of the mainline churches to the proliferation of alternative religious life-styles, with its consequence of declining church enrollments and dollars, had been taken—and it was so smooth and seemingly minor that it did not even provoke any resistance.

The Birth of the Mega-Church

About the same time, the Mega-Church also entered the religious scene with a highly attractive Christian agenda: the return to a more conservative religious environment and the sanity of control and authority. As its name implied, it was focused on ministry to a "big" audience in a super-sized church.

For people seeking a more conservative life style, this was exactly the sort of Christianity they craved. Its target audience was a growing population of the discontented who wanted to return to a more predictable and "moral" life. For those lost in the crisis and uncertainty of change, this new home offered the comfort of consistency and control.

The Mega-Church was an anchor in the deeply troubled and uncomfortable waters of challenge and change, providing many who felt adrift with rules and strategies for successful living according to conservative Christian standards.

And it grew, and grew and grew.

The creative and adaptable approach of the Mega-Church matched precisely the needs of this new audience of conservative young adults who were both spiritual seekers and had also learned about life through the (un-)reality of television. Already shaped by lessons about life served up in thirty to sixty minute segments, this new audience was programmed to be entertained.

The blitz of a hyper-intensive worship experience with vignettes on living a successful life, a rock band, and a charismatic preacher dovetailed neatly with the expectations of these young adults for high-quality entertainment—offering them the promise of a spiritual life in which problems are solved and order reigns despite the chaos all around. It was Madison Avenue on the main street of our town!

Mega-Church faith worked like a strange, new kind of drug with powerful results, reshaping the religious lives of many—but with side effects that were yet to be discovered. When television became part of the ministry of the Mega-Church, all the pieces were in place. You could attend worship in front of your television screen. You could connect to other evangelists around the country as they preached the "Word." You could pray and be healed while sitting comfortably in front of the "tube." And you could pay by credit card!

Not only were young people attracted to the substance and promises of this new message, older people who had drifted away from the church or who felt under-valued in their own church situation also found a place of identification and connection. The excitement of the worship experience, the puritan ethic dressed in new clothes, and the sense of belonging to something really successful combined as pure magic. It was a way out of the chaos. God was back in charge of the world and it was "good . . . very, very good." The Mega-Church formula seemed unbeatable!

Enter the "Psychological Church"

If the Mega-Church offered stable identities and strong moral guidance as a counter-weight to chaos, the mainstream, traditional churches turned to psychology as a behavioral antidote to "all our troubles" in the last three decades of the 20th century. What I call the "psychological church" emerged as our infatuation with this new discipline deepened. Psychology promised understanding and knowledge as keys to processing the cycles of change that were dominating our lives.

Beginning in the 1950s with the development of child psychology, a flood of information about the psychological lives of children (and proper parental behaviors to ensure appropriate growth and development) reached every household. We became "experts" in psychology because we were in the post-war mindset of trying to provide every possible advantage to our children. We were also desperate to find something . . . anything . . . that would help us cope with these powerful forces that were challenging us at every turn.

Psychology looked so promising, a shelter from the stormy blast of our out-of-control lives. But there were problems with our reliance upon it. The first problem was that we weren't "experts"; the changes were profound and unrelenting and no one was up to the task. The second problem was that psychology's answers did not reach the real question. It was a voice of rational solutions, but not a spiritual voice. It offered knowledge of human behavior, not spiritual life. In the end, when we asked psychology to solve all the problems in the family and society, it became a powerful diversion from the problems that were actually happening in the heart and spirit of the church.

As a diversion, psychology served wonderfully. We loved learning about people; we loved talking about psychological solutions to problems. A new sense of knowledge of human growth and developmental patterns comforted us. As conflicts emerged within the family and in the church, we developed strategies of "conflict management." As marriages crumbled, we developed programs of marital enrichment. As teenagers "acted out" their frustrations and confusions, we learned more about adolescent behavior. Psychology made us feel we were in control once again.

But, in reality, we were making an idol of psychology. It became a major interest in the life of the church as well as a popular mainstay in the adult education world. It was much more exciting to think we were learning how to be psychologically healthy than to concentrate on our spiritual lives. Divorced from spirituality, however, psychological answers ultimately could not sustain us.

In fact, our psychological focus (quite unintentionally) was actually preventing us from seeing the continuing loss of Spirit in our lives and in the church. It was a last ditch attempt to cure the disease that was killing our spirit, without any understanding of what was really happening.

"Pop" psychology (which had no grounding in theory, research or training) powerfully reinforced the arrival of the "Me" generation. Despite all the distinctions between the various population cohorts discussed above, the ultimate destination finally became clear: we were shifting, inexorably, both in society and in the churches, from spiritual concern for our neighbors to a concentration solely on ourselves. The world was reduced, finally, to a population of only one person. And that person was "Me"!

Clergy in the Counseling Business

In keeping with our new psychological focus, clergy were encouraged to engage in a form of counseling that resembled the discipline of psychotherapy. Historical psychic deficits; issues of self worth, depression or anger; dependence on drugs or alcohol; failing marriages; broken families; and unsatifying jobs were all grist for pastoral counseling sessions.

But the inherent risks of such well-intentioned help were not carefully considered. Many clergy lacked sufficient expertise in the complicated tasks of counseling. Issues of confidentiality were often breached despite good intentions by those who were unable to maintain privacy. The disciplines of psychology themselves were compromised on every turn by the delivery of psychological services by those who were neither trained nor supervised. Many parishioners became enamored of being important enough to meet regularly with the pastor, thereby dividing communities into an in-group and an out-group. Abuses of power and intimacy became an unexpected and tragic reality as well.

Most importantly, however, this approach reinforced the powerful shift of focus from one's spiritual life to one's psychological self. This critical problem was the one that was never addressed. Concentrating on my psychological problems left my spiritual life outside of the church. Psychological solutions to my problems eliminated the power of Spirit to transform my life. We exchanged the Mystery of being a child of God for the appearance of control; a poor exchange indeed.

The "psychological church" had triumphed.

A New Condition: Clergy Burnout

As a psychologist and minister, I was increasingly called to work with clergy who were suffering from a new condition called "clergy burnout." In their shared pain and despair, I saw the growing gulf between the gifts of ministry and the reality of life in a changing church. The loss of spiritual integrity and identity was the inevitable and visible result of ministry conducted in a survival mode.

As the world shifted, the church made Herculean efforts to keep up with the times. The effect on the clergy was a demand (often self-imposed) to work harder, with fewer satisfactions, while facing a mountain of unexpected issues they were hardly trained to address. Dealing with congregations in conflict became a major source of frustration.

Conflicts between church members; the beginnings of animosity between the local church and the distant hierarchy of the institution; and growing voices of discontent within the church membership all eroded clergy performance and competence. The call into ministry was disappearing in a morass of tasks and troubles, while clergy remained trapped in their own, as well as their congregation's, unrealistic expectations of the minister.

The experience of ministry grew more frustrating, driven by competition and the threat of failure or incompetence. The future was less assured; jobs were being threatened by the loss of members and money. A focus on one's sense of being "called" to ministry took a back seat to the reality of a "market economy" in the Church.

Heart broken, angry, disappointed and disillusioned, some clergy were doing the only thing left for them. They were leaving the church.

Economic Challenges Enter the Church

Towards the end of the 20th century, the issue of economic survival became a growing concern for the Church. Churches have to pay their bills like everyone else. The consequences of multiple issues of dissent in congregations began to be seen in declining membership roles and reduced pledges. A reduced birthrate added to the problem.

One church in western New York State had 5,000 children enrolled in its Sunday School in 1950; by 1995, there was not even one. Their classrooms, once noisy and full of life, were now only a vast, empty space. The church was reduced to attempting to rent the space to anyone who had money. And they were having difficulty doing that.

Bringing children to Sunday School is a strong factor in maintaining membership. Fewer children and more crises created an inevitable downsizing in the church's financial resources and its ability to provide ministry.

In addition, no church exists in a vacuum. In the 1990s, interest rates also began to wobble and by 2001 they crashed. Earning on endowments were thereby reduced. The church had become another institution reflecting the darkening picture of a changing economy as the new century arrived. The issue of economic survival was becoming a major issue in a growing number of households.

The Mystery of God's Presence in this world seemed trapped under the burden of survival. We wondered what else could go wrong . . . and we were right. More change was on the way.

CHAPTER 4

THE CHURCH IN FREE FALL, A WORLD IN CRISIS

*A*s we entered the 21st century, four issues challenged the future of the Mainline churches:

1. The emerging population of people looking for their spiritual life outside of the Church, e.g. multiple "new age movements";
2. The growing division in society between economic have's and have not's, including the increasing distance between churches that were experiencing growth in both numbers of members and dollars and those with shrinking financial assets and membership;
3. The increasing frustration among the clergy who were working harder than ever just to ward off the demons of change, while feeling undervalued and unappreciated for their efforts; and,
4. The powerful growth of competing institutions, such as the Mega-Church, a variety of Evangelical churches, and other religious groups including Mormons, Muslims and the Bahá'ís.

Mainline churches felt forced into a survival mode, trying different approaches and programs to preserve our spiritual identity and to compete on a new religious playing field.

However, it is difficult to "keep the faith" and to keep up with all the changes that swirl around us. If we maintain our traditions, we risk become irrelevant. If we focus on adapting to new trends, we risk neutralizing the essence of who we are. In becoming "all things" to all people, we become nothing in particular.

Evangelical, Pentecostal and African American Churches are enduring the same kinds of crises and cycles of change that Mainline churches have been facing. But these issues are more easily contained within the more structured and controlled institutional environment that characterizes these churches. And, in fact, membership in these kinds of denominations continues to grow steadily. They face different kinds of challenges.

It is also clear that the sort of upheavals we are discussing can be liberating to many (e.g., women) while at the same time troubling to those who seek to preserve older norms. More fluid and less controlled church environments are more open to the possibilities of change. If one is willing to move into and through such challenging cycles, one might just discover the possibility of new outcomes and multiple gifts.

The Facts are Finally Available

A growing number of statistics have become available to validate the decline in membership numbers in mainstream religious communities. These data also reveal the rapid growth of other kinds of religious institutions that have more tightly governed rules and regulations for membership, such as an insistence on regular conributions of both dollars and time.

A report on the shape of religious communities in the U.S. from the Hartford Institute tells us:

> The downturn in new church development in mainline Protestantism and surge in Evangelical Protestantism is familiar to most religious trend trackers. But they also should note the downturn among Roman Catholic/Orthodox and the surge in the founding of congregations among the Baha'is, Muslims and Mormons over the last 20 years. This trend is rapidly putting a new face on American religion.[4]

And, further:

> The reality, however, is that half of the religious congregations in the United States have fewer than 100 regularly participating adults and just over half are located in small town and rural settings. Indeed a full quarter of congregations has fewer than 50 regularly participating adults.[5]

As the former president of a large Protestant denomination recently shared with me: "We are all hemorrhaging." He is right! Mainline Protestant churches are facing not only a decline in funds and membership, but also in the ability to provide jobs for students graduating from seminary. In addition, many of these smaller churches are becoming churches in which the vast majority of members are growing older. Yet, as we would later discover, even the elderly are not attending church in the same numbers as they did in past eras.

Catholic and Episcopal churches struggle with their own powerful and complicated issues, facing potential schisms within their communions. Some individuals and congregations have demonstrated their power by withdrawing their financial support from those institutions whose behavior they could not tolerate or by leaving to join other churches.

In the light of the massive changes of the last fifty years, it is no wonder that institutions which regulate community life closely (e.g., the Mega-Church) have become so attractive. Active authority is a direct answer to the chaos of discomforting change, promising instead gifts of structure and permanence. But such an approach is not without cost. Within an institutional hierarchy of power and dominance, compliance and control become essential bi-products. Within a less controlled environment, the gifts of change and the diversity of people can offer opportunities not seen, and possibly not available, within a more structured environment.

Meanwhile, in the Rest of the World

All over the world, one could see and feel the agony of disharmony and conflict. Deep divisions between people echoed and enlarged what we were experiencing on our own religious landscape. Issues of change in society and the church were connected to and magnified in a world situation which appeared out of control and unsolvable.

Religious tradition pitted against opposing tradition in the Middle East brought increasing violence and destruction. Individuals and groups seeking to help the peace process were caught in the cross-fire of generations of hostility that could not be controlled.

Some argued that this was clearly the beginning stage of the end of the world. History was finally going to be decided on the Biblical battlefield of opposing forces in the Middle East. Many felt what we were seeing was a powerful and inevitable religious war between age-old factions, which had finally erupted into violence and destruction. Others remained hopeful that something could be worked out through negotiation and peaceful means of collaboration. Most people, however, simply felt helpless to change anything. The usual methods of negotiation were constantly being thwarted by new outbreaks of violence and destruction. Politics, oil reserves, boundaries, religious rage and destruction were exposed in a picture that seemed to defy any kind of solution. It was simply too big and too complicated.

For most of us, the only viable option was to retreat into some kind of passive "normalcy," trying to do business as usual, while we waited to see what was going to happen. What could we do? Not much. What should or could the church or other religious institutions be doing? Apparently, not much either. Both church and society seemed caught in a state of mutual helplessness.

When the United States became the latest victim of large-scale destruction on September 11, 2001, we found that our unquestioned sense of invincibility was toppled much like the Twin Towers. We recognized that we were as vulnerable as anyone else in the world to random tragedy. We realized that unknown, worldwide sources could execute a terrorist attack anywhere, anytime—even in a major U.S. city. No longer considered the safest country in the world, we found that living under the threat of terror was a new life experience for which we were not prepared. Our Yankee independence withered in the face of this new experience of fear. Our anxiety grew each time a new terrorist threat from a hidden enemy was announced.

It was hard to remain convinced that God was somewhere in all of this unholy anguish. It was not easy to remember that the Divine Presence is never very far from the heart of any and all situations. In fact, the single most important question we can raise in any situation that seems hopeless and out of control is always, "Where in the world is God in all of this mess?" Only by asking that question can we find an answer. But that was the one question we couldn't seem to ask. And so, God appeared to be an elusive and unpredictable Mystery in the world, visible only in random acts of profound love: prayers unexpectedly answered; healing sought and delivered; lives transformed in the midst of tragedy.

We could no longer trust that we could find God where we had grown accustomed to encountering the Divine in more stable eras. Those we had turned to in the past to identify God's Presence or Actions appeared strangely mute. We were left on our own to search—to search for something . . . anything . . . anywhere . . . anyone . . . who could speak to the urgency of our need. Meanwhile our fear was growing like the gathering of wind and waves before a storm. Voices urging us toward new kinds of spirituality were calling us to new disciplines, new behaviors. New experts arrived to tell us how to live and how to find God.

How little we understood that God was already here.

Adrift, But Not Lost

In the seismic shifts of the last fifty years, the family and community have tried to cope with rapid cycles of change that have confused and torn us from our roots and from each other. Conflicts—in the family, in our neighborhoods, in the community of nations—besieged us like ancient stories in the Bible in which conflicts and chaos abound. The weakening of our strong religious anchors had cast us adrift from our most sustaining and comforting values.

But what we have been experiencing is not the loss of the presence of God in this world and not the loss of our direct connection to God. It is the breaking open of new avenues of awareness and connection that can be discovered precisely in those moments when life collapses around us and God appears to be remote or inaccessible. The cycles of change that are propelling us into the future bring with them the ongoing promises of God to be with us and to become "real" in our lives in new and unexplainable ways.

In Christian terms, the death and resurrection of Jesus Christ is the reality of that promise. The spiritual solution to the uncertainties of our unfolding new world is to discover the Mystery and Love of God revealed in the very center of our existence whenever "change" becomes the medium for "New Life."

We turn now to three new models of church and ministry that can serve as examples of God's generous, surprising Living Presence in the world. Each of these "churches" began and grew during times of upheaval and challenge precisely because "God became Real" in each one.

May these stories speak to your heart and spirit that you might discover their messages of transformation and hope.

PART TWO

A CHURCH IN THE GYM:
FINDING GOD IN
UNEXPECTED PLACES

CHAPTER 5

DISCOVERING GOD'S OTHER NAME

Within the last fifty years of change just described, one additional reality has broken open and challenged our standard attempts to define and locate God. As the facts pour in, the evidence clearly points toward an indisputable truth: God has another name, and that name is "Surprise"!

Far from being absent from this world, we have only to look at our lives to discover God's surprising presence: an unexpected event; a turning in a new direction; a crisis that contained a gift; a moment when life suddenly shifts and plans must be abandoned. Learning to see God's presence as catalytic in moments of change and surprise brings us to the basic grounding of our spiritual lives: God is everywhere! God is real in the very center of life. God is as close as our next breath. God is with each of us, wherever we happen to be, 24/7. Such moments of recognition, or what I like to call "God Surprises," contain new life and new possibilities in whatever situation they occur. The Gifts of God are available to everyone. Recognizing and receiving them ignites the possibilities they contain!

My life was no exception.

My First God Surprise

I've loved almost everything about the Church since I was a young child. The sights and sounds of the Church fill my spirit. Even when I go into an empty church, I am touched and transported to some other place and time that often brings me to tears. Scripture, sacraments and ceremonies all open the depth of my being to the presence of God in the world. But the thought of becoming a minister of the Church never crossed my mind nor entered my life planning. At that time in my life, I'd never even seen a clergywoman; let alone talked to one. It was out of the question. I had my own future plans, ones that put God in church, not in the center of my life.

SURPRISE! Enter God with another agenda. One day, without pronouncement, advance warning or permission, God became real in my life. I was 32 years of age. The year was 1963 and my life was about to be transformed.

I was cleaning house. My two older children were in school; the youngest was upstairs asleep. It was naptime and so I was doing all those things that mothers do while the kids are safely tucked away. An ordinary day. I don't remember the exact date, but it was in the spring. I had no premonitions that this day would be different from any other. I was methodically dusting the bookshelves: taking the books, one by one, off the shelf, and dusting front, back and around the pages in an accustomed rhythm that required no thinking. "Doing it right," as my mother would have said.

We had several Bibles stored on the shelves. They were dusty from lack of use—not that I wasn't a church-goer, just not much of a Bible reader. On this particular day, I lifted one of the Bibles off the shelf and performed my dusting ritual. Instead of putting it back into its allotted slot, I put it on the dining room table. Inexplicably, I opened it—not to the first page, but to a place toward the back, not to a specific passage but a simple gesture of opening.

I read the words at the beginning of the text, rather than scanning the whole page as I might ordinarily do. I read the same words a second time. On the third reading, my life, as I knew it, ended. A new life had begun for me, jumpstarted by seventeen celestial words that simultaneously opened my heart and flooded my spirit with the Presence of God:

In the beginning was the Word,
And the Word was with God
And the Word was God (John 1:1).

Time stopped. The world shifted ever so slightly, revealing a space in which only God and I were present. In that milli-second of time, I somehow knew I had experienced God. I knew exactly who Jesus was. I knew I would never again be the same person who had casually opened the Bible while dusting my bookshelf.

I couldn't explain my experience . . . not at all. I just knew. How did I know? I had no words to describe what had happened. All I knew was that God had been present and that God was now in charge of my life, not me. The message had arrived and I received it. My spirit came to life!

Entering God Space and God Time

After reading those opening words of John's gospel on that spring day, I felt as if I had entered a new spiritual dimension of life called "God Space and God Time." I was now living a dual existence; I lived both in the ordinary reality of my everyday life and in the reality of the Spirit where everything was entirely unexpected and unplanned.

Only once did I try to explain what had happened to a friend. From her response, it was clear that she thought I had lost my mind or had become one of those "crazy religious people." After that, I placed my experience into the center of my heart and let it grow there, protected from interference or question.

Whenever we enter "God Space and Time," all the rules change. God supplies a new "medium" for our life and invites us to "look" around and see everything in a new light. Nothing felt forced. Instead, I felt like I had just received an invitation to enter a world filled with unexpected surprises. What I discovered was a marvelous new landscape—the same people and the same world—but now in dazzling Technicolor, where before it was only black and white.

For the next thirty years, I would learn that God is always present in this world. Our connection to God is permanent and irrevocable. We both know this and don't know it. We learn this truth, but we also forget it. We must learn it again and again. When we do, we are overwhelmed by God's Presence in our lives. In such moments, we know once again that we are full participants in God's Loving Mission in this world, connected and held by the Divine Mystery, and brought into new life as a new creation. I think about it as akin to what a baby experiences in the process of exiting from the womb and entering the world: of having one's life supports suddenly "unplugged" but, at the same time, being washed, blanketed and cradled in the warmth of arms, bodies, sounds and love. Connecting to God is a journey from inside-out, from old to new, from birth to life.

A Surprising Call into Ministry

It wasn't long before "surprise" became the hallmark of my life. Whether a breakthrough in my creative life or that most significant surprise of a call into the ministry, surprises abounded. Never planned, never sought, never expected. God kept showing up and leading me forward.

In the 1960s, very few women took up space in the seminary. Women were not unfamiliar with seminary life. A few courageous women fought the good fight and entered the ministry in the 1800s. More continued to enter seminaries in the first half of the 20th century. But men clearly dominated the clergy-world up until the mid-20th century and women were not encouraged to challenge that reality. A few, liberal seminaries welcomed, with varying degrees of enthusiasm, the few women who applied for admission to seminary; the conservative institutions locked and bolted their doors against the intrusion of female candidates. Some believed it was inappropriate for women to be clergy and mothers at the same time. Others denied the possibility that women had the skills and intelligence for ministry. In the reactive language of the 1960s, it was "too much, too soon" for women to challenge the church hierarchy with their presence and their wish for equal status.

My newly incarnated life had been birthed in a season of change. But the truth of my call into ministry would not go away in spite of powerful challenges to my decision. Fed by an invisible and living source of spiritual energy, it never wavered or diminished.

However, when I approached my senior pastor with my wish to go to seminary, he said flat out: "Women don't belong in the ministry. I won't support your going to seminary. You'll have to convince the church because I won't have anything to do with your call!" Then, as if to soften the blow he had just struck to my spirit, he added: "You could become a Director of Christian Education. Yes, that's the right path for you." He smiled with satisfaction as if he had solved a problem that was more an annoyance than a challenge. But, as I understood God's call, I resisted his suggestion. It was not easy. Earlier in my life, I would have "done the right thing" and acceded to his request. But, surprise again—a spirit of power and courage. I said "no!" Another brand new experience.

A local Methodist Seminary reluctantly opened its doors to me as a "special student." This meant I had one year to prove I was really serious about going into ministry. God prevailed. I finished seminary and was ordained in 1970 as one of two women in a graduating class of over forty.

Still, I was publicly pronounced a "non-unanimous candidate for ministry." Clearly, this was only round one!

Immediately, a new "surprise" arrived in the form of an invitation to become a graduate student in a doctoral program in counseling psychology at a neighboring university—all expenses paid, including a monthly stipend for the duration of the degree and a chance to teach. This gift had "God" written all over it. Asking no questions, I said "Yes" immediately.

Then I waited for the next gift to arrive. I didn't have to wait long.

Into the Fire of Ministry

Once again, God stirred the pot. This time it was the women from a large United Church of Christ (UCC) congregation who served as God's agents in the world. They hired me to be their part-time woman pastor, to serve their needs in new and creative ways. I could start my ministry and continue my doctoral program in psychology at the same time. It seemed like a marriage made in heaven. But the consequences of this decision created a powerful backlash in the church.

The women's plan was to hire their own minister, which they undertook without permission or approval of the governing body of the church. For them, it was simple. They would write my contract and pay my salary; I would serve as their pastor. It was also remarkable: The growing empowerment of women in the late 1960s who came to life in an ordinary church environment in a quiet suburban world!

It may have been simple and remarkable, but the idea was not well-received by all. Some interpreted the plan to imply that I could not minister to any non-females in the congregation, creating a challenge to the very core of ministry in a local church. Could you actually hire a minister to be pastor of only a portion of the congregation? Could a sub-group in a church choose to govern and support its own minister? As in all desperate and messy situations, the surprises of God waited to be discovered in the very heart of the conflict.

Breaking all the rules of ministry by being hired by approximately two-thirds of the congregation; seen as a hostile intruder by some of the other third (and, in fact, a few of the original two-thirds as well); described as sneaking under the "tent" to get into a church position; dressing inappropriately by wearing pink shoes in a worship service, I was given absolute freedom in my ministry because no one knew quite how to get rid of me.

The Surprise of a Divided Church

In the 1960s, seminaries were not completely insulated from the rapidly changing societal norms and values that we have highlighted above. In fact, some seminaries attempted to move with the changing secular scene, creating new models of ministry. Others held tight to the old standards of authority and control. The arrival of women clergy fanned the flames of change into an undeniable and visible reality that was definitely not going to go away!

Ecclesiastical control and authority were surely challenged by those audacious women who dared to find their own minister and insisted on hiring her themselves. "Damn the torpedoes, full speed ahead!" could have served as their motto. They remained steadfast and unflinching as strong resistance to my presence in the church began to grow.

It was as if all the frustration and anxiety wrought by the all the change occurring in the general society suddenly focused on the unacceptable entrance of one woman into a church situation, without permission. Boundaries of authority had been challenged. Women had left their "place." Established processes for the selection and hiring of ministers had been cast aside and ignored. The residue of unfinished conflicts in the church rose to the surface and divided the congregation in two: the old guard versus the new challengers.

To this naive, neophyte minister just out of seminary, the discovery of the divided church exposed the harsh reality of embattled congregations. The lengths to which people went to express their displeasure with the clergy—from petty gossip to projections of distrust and rejection to mounting campaigns to force ministers to resign—showed me a picture of congregational life I had never expected to see. This was the church in a mode of struggle and survival, competition and closed door conspiracies, commonly known as "church politics."

In response to these negative behaviors, people would often say, "That's just the way it is. Institutions foster power struggles and petty behaviors." Usually, such statements are accompanied by a visible shrug which seems to add, "Dummy! Why would you expect anything else? The Church is made up of people, and people in institutions always have these problems." But such passivity and acquiescence is not helpful. The issue may be closed, but it is not resolved, only tabled until the next uproar arrives.

I didn't buy such explanations nor was I willing to believe this was the end of the story. After all, if the Church is just like every other institution in this world, why go there? Where in the world was God in such a setting? Or, why bother with God if such petty "church politics" are inevitable? If this is true, then the God of Creative Unexpected Surprise, the Generous Provider of New Life, would have disappeared entirely from the scene. There had to be more to this picture than what I was seeing.

All it took for me to find God's answer to all this conflict was to teach an adult education class in the basement of the church. Another surprise awaited!

A Church in a Gym?

My "adult education" class was assigned to the church gym—in the basement. Underneath the "church proper," in a space bathed in sunshine from rows of large windows, with basketball hoops at either end, and a few folding chairs stacked for seating in the corner, a Church in the Gym came to life.

In this basement, I found people hungry for the opportunity to share their lives with each other, people eager to open internal channels to God's presence, people ready to share tears and hugs; people ready to care. This unlikely space became filled to overflowing with the wonderful energy of Spirit.

A church beyond petty politics was, in fact, quite easy to find. This "other" church began when a group of individuals and couples of all ages simply wandered into that open space, looked around, and wondered what was coming next. Right on time, Spirit arrived to transform us all. Together, we became novitiates in a new kind of ministry, built not with hierarchies of power, but in the encounter of people with people and in the discovery of our connection with God as we learned how to connect with each other. In that gym, God became Real for every one of us!

I found a new "God Space and God Time" right in the heart of this conflict-ridden church. While a portion of the congregation may have been embattled, I met a small, non-political, harmonious, spirit-filled "small church" within it—a space and time where people gathered, simply, to talk about life. In the process of being together, we discovered God present—not in the sanctuary on Sunday morning, but in the gym. And, encountering God in the basement, we began to notice God in the parking lot, on the street, around kitchen tables—God present at any hour, in any place, wherever two or three gathered to share their lives. The Spirit of God available to transform our lives twenty four hours a day, seven days a week.

In this small crucible of extraordinary/ordinary people, the meaning of ministry came to life for me. I discovered an ongoing, dynamic and continuous connection between God, the people of God, and life, operating both within and outside of the church. In these gatherings, in our Church in the Gym, we received the gift of God's Presence in our lives; we shared that gift with others and we returned to our community to deepen our spiritual connection and begin again. It was that simple.

A Church in the Gym became a sanctuary of ordinary, yet sacred, shared moments of life, intermingled with the sounds of relief and laughter in the discovery of our common humanity. Communion shared in the gym was a holy time of healing for the spirit and an affirmation of God's Presence. These were all God gifts—not pre-packaged from my training for ministry, but moments of deep, unexpected connection in which we all grew.

Connecting Community, God and Life

The role of the community was central to the life of the Church in the Gym. Together, we learned that God is not bound to particular buildings nor to specific times. Instead, Church occurs whenever two or three gather to talk about God, to share life understanding and experiences and to enter into a process of transformation in which God becomes real. In other words, our Church in the Gym was grounded in the reality of God present in each moment—not in the gym itself or in those adult education sessions. It could occur anytime, anywhere, under any condition, for anyone.

The key to the whole process was the vitality and energy that grew as we established the connection between God and life. When we spoke of our lives, we were simultaneously looking for God in those lives. As we understood God as the great Surprise, as transforming Spirit, we were also experiencing the power of the community to affirm and transmit that message to others.

Ordinarily, in a church setting, new members are integrated into the community by being encouraged to join a committee so as to get acquainted with other people and the church body as a whole. In other words, we give people a job and assume that will help them to feel incorporated; we start with the business of the church and hope we can get to God.

In the Church in the Gym, we made no such assignments. Instead, we simply talked to one another about God and our lives—our marriages, our families, our relationships, our jobs, and so on. Through such ordinary human lenses, we came to experience God in the center of our community.

In that sort of setting, a different group process emerges. When God is the center of a group experience, issues of separation and judgment disappear. God's Spirit entered our space, not in some forced or contrived manner, but shared in the flesh of our experiences brought into the context of God's acknowledged presence.

Eventually, my army of support, those audacious women of the church who continued to brandish their swords of freedom and love, won their battle and I was hired by all, to do ministry for all. As satisfying as that outcome was, the Church in the Gym had already changed my life and transformed the future course of my ministry.

CHAPTER 6

THE GIFTS AND LESSONS OF
THE CHURCH IN THE GYM

We learned simple and profound truths in our time together in the gym. These truths were more unspoken, that is we didn't catalogue them in a list of stages, steps or action plans. Instead, they were part of our connection with God. We understood the Presence of God because we were experiencing it.

Our agenda was to talk about life in its most ordinary forms, and to discover God present in that experience. We listened carefully to each other and took what we were learning out into the world with us. Our outside mission became as important as our experience of being together in the gym.

We studied a variety of Biblical and other resources. We delighted in the richness of laughter and we cried when our hearts were touched and moved. The presence of God simply grew with us, without our taking any steps to make that happen.

Lessons Learned

Our shared experiences brought us to a deeper understanding of the ongoing Mystery of God, particularly in times of profound change. Together, we learned that God is always present whenever we acknowledge God in life. We came to understand that the role of the church is to be a mirror and vehicle for that discovery. We learned a new model of church:

- Church begins when two or three people gather to talk about life;
- Church takes place whenever, wherever, or however this happens;
- Church includes everyone who chooses to be there;
- Church occurs when we recognize God in the midst of our lives and start to live life with God at the center of everything;
- Transformation is possible when God and life become interconnected, when God becomes real in the midst of our lives; and,
- Taking our spiritual gifts into the world is essential to the process.

The power of the community in connection with God and each other enabled us to share our experiences and questions. We each learned to speak in an open venue in which God became even more real and available. For most of us, it was the first time we had experienced that freedom.

"Church in the Gym" became code words to express the reality that we can trust the emerging processes of change as part of God's faithful ministry to us. With that understanding, those powerful and sometimes precarious cycles of change could also be seen as "mustard seeds" of transformation and new life. Changes, even uncomfortable ones, were not to be feared but could be entered into as an opportunity to discover God's Spirit in a new setting. Birthed in a time of upheaval in the world outside, our Church in the Gym grew as we accepted that change also carries with it the possibilities of surprise and connection.

For Christians, our "resurrection faith" allows us to see that new life always emerges out of death, out of change or loss. Events may not proceed as we may have imagined or planned or expected, but each loss, each change is an opportunity to see new life emerging out of the chaotic, disturbing and sometimes frightening moments of an unknown future. In theological language, change provides an opportunity to know once again the deepest meanings of the life, death and resurrection of Jesus.

What We Actually Did

The Church in the Gym followed a simple structure.

1. We met weekly on Sunday mornings in the adult education slot between church services.
2. The agenda for the meeting followed a flow of life issues, church related or not, which were presented and then examined to identify how God was present in these aspects of our lives.
3. Discussion and interaction were an essential part of the experience and always spontaneous in nature—not argumentative, judgmental or dogmatic. We were all learners and listeners (clergy included).
4. Our direction moved consistently from life to the question of "where is God in this situation?" In other words, we began with life issues, and moved toward the discovery of God in those issues. So often, we start with God and never get to life. But God and life are "intermarried." You can't have one without the other.
5. Talking to others about the nature of our discoveries was a necessary and critical action for the group. If we had remained focused only on receiving these gifts and blessings for ourselves, the Spiritual energy and integrity of the experience would have begun to dry up. Our message was our mission to the world. You can't keep it to yourself.
6. We focused on one essential message: God is real and present to all people in all places and at all times. The God we met in the church gym was the same God everywhere. When God becomes real, in whatever place or time, new life always begins.

Out of the Gym, into the World

After nearly a decade together, it was clearly time to take the gifts and lessons we had been given into the world outside of the gym, without knowing exactly when, where or what that might mean. What we did know was that our experience in the gym created a new vision and mission for the church. Not unlike an adolescent growing into adulthood, our vision needed to be tested in the world. It could not remain in its comfortable home, as an untried dream only to be forgotten later. It needed to have the opportunity to grow in new and different environments.

We collected a new series of questions. Did a "Church in the Gym" exist in other settings? Could a "church in two parts" be united in its mutual strength and awareness of God in each moment? Would God become Real in any community that acknowledged God's presence? But to find our answers, we had to leave the safety of our sanctuary in the gym and allow our vision to grow and change. All growth challenges our strength and our ability to trust in the unknown. It relies on our readiness to say an unqualified and unrestricted "Yes" to the voice of God's Spirit speaking to our spirit, without knowing where that Spirit will lead us. Learning to trust in the dark is one of God's special, perhaps favorite, gift.

The experiences of nearly a decade of experiencing God in a church gym were placed in a backpack of gifts and visions to become a Mission on the move. It was time to leave the safety of the gym and enter the world.

Once again, we were in for quite a surprise.

PART THREE

A CHURCH WITHOUT WALLS:
DISCOVERING AN UNEXPECTED
INTERFAITH WORLD

CHAPTER 7

THE NEW CHURCH: REINVENTING MINISTRY

Within a few months and through many prayerful conversations with interested others, "The New Church: A Caring Community" quietly made its entry into the outside world as an extension of the Church in the Gym. Two lessons learned in the gym became the vision and mandate for the New Church: first, Church happens whenever and wherever two or three are gathered to talk about God, to share their lives and to take these transforming gifts into the world; and, second, God becomes Real and present to us whenever we acknowledge God's Presence. In essence, we were simply carrying a new vision for ministry and mission to the larger, struggling Church, within a community environment devoted to caring.

Our mission evolved as an experimental ministry to the Church at large. This unusual mission allowed us to examine critical issues the Church was facing in a new and different context without having to "fix" them. Instead, we could look at these situations as a crucible in which we might see new opportunities for change: new models of ministry, new roles for the community, new forms of worship, and new ways in which the community might find its spiritual identity.

We understood our new, larger landscape as an open field of possibilities rather than a spiritual desert devoid of life and energy. We anchored ourselves in the constant and caring presence of God and began our new adventure.

Getting Started

The practical dimensions of The New Church emerged as we answered a series of basic questions: Where should we meet? When should we meet? How should we gather the community? What in the world will we do?

The answer of "where to meet" and "when to meet" joined together as our first critical decision. Nothing would happen without finding a place and setting a time. Enter God and the Wilmette Masonic Temple, which was then occupied by a group of Masons, a small Jewish congregation, a Lutheran community, and the Fine Arts

Quartet, who recorded their music in this acoustically marvelous space. There was ample room for everyone and the Temple turned out to be vacant on Friday evenings for a very modest rental fee. We solved our where and when. We rented the temple for a six-month trial period, beginning on the first Friday evening of May 1979.

The question of "what would we do?" took us back into our roots. Sharing a meal was part of our Christian heritage. The temple contained both a large meeting room and a marvelous kitchen designed to service groups. We could break bread in the same space where we would worship. This felt exactly right. God had provided a first step.

The question of "how to gather the community" was turned over to God. We did not advertise. We did not solicit "members." We chose, instead, to let the Spirit guide the selection process. Our doors were open to anyone of any age and any persuasion to share a meal and see what would develop. Everyone was welcome.

Since we met on Friday evenings rather than Sunday mornings, we hoped any concerns about our drawing members from local churches would be minimal. In fact, throughout its 25 year life span as a community, over 80% of our community continued to retain their membership at (and attend) their home church or synagogue while also being a part of The New Church. (The remaining 20% didn't have a home church or synagogue to attend.)

Word of mouth created The New Church: A Caring Community. Twice a month we gathered with God as our Host: once on the first Friday of the month for dinner and worship and once mid-week during the month to reinforce our growing connections with God and each other. In a simple and very basic format, we prayed, learned from each other, celebrated Communion, and followed the Christian liturgical year.

The New Church belonged to God and to everyone who brought their hearts, lives and spirits to it. Caring for God, each other and the world around us provided our reason for being. Whatever the future contained, we were content to let it unfold.

It's About Spirit, Not Survival

Without a building to support and repair or a staff to pay, we entered a different economic world. The focus shifted from survival to spirit and the powerful experience of being a God-directed community, open to whatever processes might emerge from our experiences together.

In fact, when God acts as the producer, director and chief actor in this new kind of play called "church" (or, perhaps, this new kind of church called "play") marvelous, unexpected things can happen.

A New Model for Ministry and Worship

When one looks for alternative models of ministry, one sees with even greater clarity the overburdened life of many contemporary clergy, especially as economic struggles result in longer work hours, fewer associates with whom to share ministry, and less resources to support one's work. One quickly sees a picture of a vocation that has stress and exhaustion written all over it.

To combat some of the problems of clergy burnout, our vision called for the community to take a much more active role in the ministry of the church. In the informal, non-traditional, open-ended environment of the New Church, we first initiated changes in ministry by simply raising the activity level of the congregation through direct participation in the worship service.

Put simply, during worship, we broke regularly into smaller groups to talk and write about some specific assignment and then returned to the larger group to share our wisdom. Each assignment developed the theme of the interconnection between God and life, whether played out in the Bible or in some other historical or contemporary resource. A multitude of voices and experiences responded.

This "ministry of many" formed a cohesive center, which operated to relieve the pastor of some of the responsibilities of ministry. More often than not, the congregation had more creative, playful, and insightful ideas about "spiritual" issues than the pastor. It was wonderful.

Our worship was profoundly simple and the core of our life together. We prayed and ate; learned about God and life and shared our communion meal. We went our separate ways filled with our mission to bring our experiences in some way into the world. No one was obliged to participate. Questions and comments were entirely welcomed. Silence was frequently observed. Tears and laughter were special gifts.

Devoting two evenings a month to sharing the life of the Spirit filled us with the gifts of community and connection. God was real in the past; real in the present; and real in the moment at our table and in our worship. We rarely left our meeting hungry.

We had become a new kind of church.

The "Ministry of the Many" Enriches Worship

The shared ministry in the New Church became a powerful tool to level the playing field of differences in the community, creating a mutual sense of equality, respect, and responsibility. New people sensed this and felt immediately at home. The unordained clergy had powerful stories to tell about the presence and action of God in their lives. By virtue of sheer numbers, they had more spirit, energy and heart to bring to the community than I did as the one ordained person in a system of many. What a gift to be one ordinary person in the spiritual company of others!

The more the congregation claimed its own "priesthood" the more energy and vitality were present in worship. The more vulnerability shared by the pastor, the more open and responsible the group became. Worship as a community activity filled the room with the Spirit of God, present and active, not rooted in one person, but echoing throughout the community.

Our worship life anchored our church.

The Power of Shared Leadership

The issue of who holds the power in any system can become deeply divisive. When power struggles happen between laity and clergy, multiple agendas appear and the entire church becomes a battlefield. Ultimately everyone feels "powerless" and disabled. But power even modestly relinquished by one person in authority (e.g., the minister) can open the door to a shared leadership system, which has a healthy ripple effect through out the system (church or otherwise). In other words, shared power opens the door to the Spirit in our midst. Tightly held power creates animosity and resentment and closes the door to Spirit.

It's a little like what happens in families when pre-adolescents become teenagers. The family engages in a power struggle as parents and children redefine the roles and responsibilities of family members. The locus of power and authority needs to shift and broaden to accommodate the growth of a new generation and a new family structure.

Shared leadership in the church engages people at a spiritual level and creates an open space for transformation. When people operate as a priesthood of all believers, they are looking at ways the entire community can express the presence of God. The responsibility and humanity of the whole system can grow.

Shared leadership does not mean that no one is in charge. It means that everyone has a stake in what happens to the community.

Mutual respect is the container that makes shared leadership possible. Mutual respect also creates a deepened sense of self-respect. And, not surprisingly, self-respect is always a direct antidote to feeling powerless.

Caring as a Spiritual Identity

Caring has always been a part church life, expressed in the multiple ways church members help others in the church and in the community at large. Almost all churches have groups of people who participate in ministries of care, whether in altar guilds, which maintain the sanctuary; as Sunday School teachers; or, as people who call on the infirm and the elderly. The list goes on and on.

We brought the issues of "caring" into this spiritual church's name itself: The New Church: A Caring Community. "Caring" stood at the core of our community life, expressed in every interaction. In effect, we took on the issue of "caring" to find out what it might mean in a new and different setting of the church.

Naming "caring" as the focus of the church and ministry, we learned that caring also means to bring out the best of who we are in every situation. Caring, then, becomes a highly participatory experience that requires an action level well beyond a simple sense of liking or being fond of others. At the core of caring, there is a quality of "devotion" which is always a direct link to the Divine.

Devotion involves active caring without expecting anything in return. It is a gift that grows as it is used because it doesn't require a reinforcement or response to continue. It is both self reflective (this is who I am) and self-reinforcing (this is who I choose to be). It means being all that I am and discovering even more about myself in the process.

Devotion, freely given, is a transforming experience. It grows us into people who have become directly connected to the power and presence of God. All of our tasks of devotion directly mirror God's devotion to us. We become interconnected to the Divine Creator through the deeply moving, ever growing process of devotion.

Devotion in a church brings the Mystery of God directly into the community. As a self-less activity, it is directly antithetical to the claim of power and control. Instead, one discovers how to transmit the loving messages of our Creator God directly into the lives of the people without expectations of reward.

The amazing effectiveness of devotion is seen most directly in the release of power issues. Devotion and power cannot even exist in the same room because they are polar opposites. Devotion leads to the presence of the Divine. Power can dance on the edge of the demonic.

God's Surprises Continue

The changes we sought to discover were now in place. A new model for church and worship expanded into a new model for shared ministry in the community. Caring became a model for devotion expressed within and outside of the community and provided our spiritual identity. All these changes came to life with a naturalness that was both familiar and new. But none of us were prepared for the surprises that God had in store for us as we would become an interfaith congregation of Protestants, Catholics and Jews worshiping together in a Christian context, and meeting at a Masonic Temple. An entirely open and inclusive community.

For the next twenty five years, from 1979 to 2004, The New Church's mission would run on a parallel track with the changes in the rest of the world. It was a gift of constancy and simplicity in the middle of a shifting universe centered in being a new caring community with God entirely in charge. Our Church in the Gym had become a New Church without the walls of limitations, restrictions or territories. A place for everyone had been established. We had found a way to gather very diverse groups of people and establish a community of faith in which each of our differences were essential to the life and depth of the church.

We had much to be thankful for and to celebrate. Praise God!

CHAPTER 8

CHALLENGES AND GIFTS IN
THE NEW CHURCH:
PRACTICES THAT SUSTAIN
COMMUNITY

Throughout the life of The New Church, the format for our monthly Friday night worship service remained constant. At its most basic level, we had a three-part celebration: our meal, the worship service and communion. The central element, the worship service, was based on spiritual reflections and experiences presented in a theological framework. The meaning of our meal and our rite of communion further developed our spiritual understanding and identity.

Sharing Our Meal

Eating together was an important symbol of the New Church. Our meal reminded us of the gifts and blessings of being together and the opportunity to share this worship time. Eating brought us pleasure and respite, allowing us to survive, stop working and be re-energized.

The mythology of the "water hole" reminds us that when animals come to a water hole to satisfy their thirst and their real life needs for nourishment, they "agree" to cease and desist from fighting around the water hole. Whether this is pure folk fiction or biological fact, the idea is that we recognize our mutual need for life sustenance and can lay down our animosities and our swords briefly in recognition that everyone, even an enemy, has the right to meet life's necessities.

Sharing our food opened our worship, allowing us to receive replenishment of our spirits. There are at least three kinds of food necessary to nourish full human life—physical, relational and spiritual. We need to eat to be healthy but, so too, the food of relationship is essential to our lives. Without water and food, we would die; without spiritual food, we become like the walking dead.

Our meal constituted the opening act of our worship. Three members of our community brought their care and devotion to our "table," providing us with the food of nourishment for our bodies. Sharing our meal prepared us to replenish our connections with each other.

The "Food" of Worship

Our worship, grounded in community participation, defined the church as one body, filled with many parts, each essential to the health of the body. Biblical and theological resources, as well as resources from literature and life, provided the food of our worship and the stimulus for our assignments and discussions. Together, we learned about God in the world, about God's presence in our individual lives. Following the liturgical calendar brought us the constancy and structure of cycles of stories of God's presence throughout history. Without the usual pillars in a sanctuary to hide behind or the other devices we use to make ourselves hidden, we were entirely visible to each other and could directly experience our lives and wisdom as a community.

The New Church established a new form of worship that could be replicated anywhere people gathered. Eating together, learning together, sharing our Christian Communion created a total experience of care and devotion. We grew as the Spirit led us to grow.

The Blessing of Communion

We ended our worship time with a communion celebration, which honored and proclaimed the life, death and resurrection of Jesus, both in the past and in the present moment. Jesus' message of New Life acknowledged the spiritual reality and nourishment of our community and became the symbol we used before we went back into the world.

The food at the beginning of our worship allowed us to leave the world of work and gather as a community. It filled and prepared us to receive our worship service. The communion meal at the end focused us on the blessings, gifts and mystery of God and filled us with the spiritual energy to take those gifts of God back into the world.

Life and worship, enclosed within these two simple and visible realities of nourishment, became joined as one essential unit: Life as Worship and Worship as Life, bracketed by the realities of living and the mystery of God present. A circle of simple wholeness touched the depth of our collective being, heart, spirit and body. We were joined to God and to life as we were joined to each other in the wholeness of our worship experience.

Refusing to Play the Numbers Game

In most churches, the challenge of numbers interrupts the pursuit of spiritual life with the very basic issue of money and the economic health of the institution. Most churches require money to pay the pastor(s); money for maintenance and repair of the church; money for programs; money to promote growth; and so on. Money needs are an ever-present reality in church as well as life. Yet meeting such needs is complicated and can be exhausting.

Having to play the numbers game can numb the lives of many clergy, sapping their spiritual energy and integrity. Numbers become the omnipotent measure of success or failure and place all clergy under the unholy umbrella of competition and survival. If you have enough numbers—enough members, enough programs, enough cash, enough endowment—you are judged to be a success among your fellow clergy and in the hierarchy of the Church. However, success depends upon the continuation of good numbers and so it has no inherent guarantees. One cannot grow complacent or rest. Competition is as powerful a reality in the Church as in any other institution—and it never ends. If, in contrast, your numbers are low, you lose stature, risking being marked as a failure. The resultant anxiety and stress become intolerable. Numbers not only define who we are as clergy, they become a means to judge our success in our chosen profession and can determine our survival in ministry.

Reflecting on the numbers game points to a larger question: Is the Church a "business" or not? If it's a business that happens to be a church, then it can be appropriately judged by the standards of business. If, however, it's a church that is looking for different ways to examine the issue of money, then you have a new opportunity to define what church is all about.

In The New Church, in keeping with our agenda of newness, we looked for different ways to transpose the issue of money and numbers into a new context. We certainly had money needs: rent to pay, food to purchase, some kind of support for the minister. However, because I am also a clinical psychologist with other means of revenue, the question of support for the minister could be somewhat flexible. We made do with what we had. It was pretty simple. My salary became the dependent variable.

This kind of hand-to-mouth system of money management would be unacceptable in the usual church setting. Yet, there are some interesting arguments in its favor to consider. For instance, it encourages the minister to have another source of employment and income, and thereby enables the minister to operate from a less controlled and powerless place in the church. For the community, it means having less of the pastor's available time and forces so the community to take on more of the tasks of ministry. But, as we noted above, this can be a win/win for everyone as the pastor and the community combine their efforts to accomplish the work of the church, reinforcing their shared ministry and mission to be God's Caring People.

The New Church as a Spiritual Half-Way House

God's gifts and surprises continued to arrive. After our first year or two of operation, people began to appear at our doorstep who were damaged in some way by their original church experience and had left that church home, feeling separated and disconnected. Rarely did they give us the details, but clearly what remained in their heart was a hunger for some kind of spiritual experience accompanied by a wariness as to whether any religious community could give them what they wanted.

Word of mouth brought these seekers to us, with a mixture of curiosity and longing that allowed them the courage to step once more into a religious environment. We asked no questions. They ate and grew with us. Most stayed.

More surprises continued to appear. A small number of declared Catholics, Episcopalians, and Presbyterians began a pilgrimage with us. Along with them came an equal number of people who had spent only a brief time in a church setting. These folks were essentially unchurched, but they were also hungry for something spiritual. Because there were no rules for membership, no exclusionary practices, no demands for active participation, and no thoughts about numbers, all were welcomed to simply partake of the generosity of God and the celebration of community. Blessedly, people were left alone to simply take in and explore the experience. And they thrived.

We came to understand this new role as a "Spiritual Half Way House" as another unexpected gift from God's divine Grace. We could serve as a spiritual home for anyone wanting simply to enter a God-directed experience and see what would happen. Our gatherings functioned as a time of respite and renewal with no forced or premature decisions of membership or commitment.

As the name, "half way house," suggests, we were also engaged in a nurturing ministry. We helped to prepare people to go out into the world, having been nourished and sustained by the connections they had made with God and a community of caring people who valued their differences and loved their presence.

A New Gift: The Opportunity to Bridge Faith Traditions

When the first Jewish visitors came into our unabashedly Christian experience, we discovered unexpected spiritual connections among us. Some of these new friends felt disenfranchised within the life of their Temple. Others, although born Jewish, had never really connected to their faith tradition. They remained on the outside of a tradition, even as it was still a vital part of their identity. They described themselves as Jewish, but were living without a connection to sustain their spiritual lives. They felt welcomed in the openness and acceptance of our community. They began to listen and experience what we were about and to absorb the freedom and respect that was visible in the community. They decided to stay.

Our Jewish friends were able to speak their views, raise their questions, experience our Christian worship (including communion), and retain their Jewish citizenship in their own faith tradition. In other words, we lived together within these traditional divides and simply engaged in a common devotion to the one God of both of our faith traditions.

When Catholics arrived at our worship, they seemed to find a new form of Catholicism within the openness of our worship setting. Having lived their lives in a more restricted religious environment, they especially enjoyed the exploration of faith in the open sharing of one's spirit and life within the community. We spoke words and scriptures heretofore unspoken in their experiences as Catholics. They were like children who had suddenly discovered a new and marvelous toy that they could touch, feel, hold and explore without interference or guilt. They found new life among us—and they stayed.

And, so, The New Church became an interfaith Christian community—a wonderfully unexpected, and particularly unique, gift from God indeed. We did not give up our Christian identity. We referenced Christ as our model for life and served communion at each worship service. But we did not limit ourselves to one tradition either. We used Protestant, Catholic and Jewish resources as part of the liturgy of our community. Sharing prayer texts from our various traditions brought us closer to each other, but they also showed us the richness of traditions we were missing by living separate spiritual lives.

Without plans and strategies, we were becoming an interfaith community of highly diverse people who were integrating themselves into one community.

We were eating at the same spiritual table.

A Church of the Revolving Door

While we marveled at our spiritual "halfway house" status and our interfaith community, God passed another gift into our corporate lives. After spending a few years with us, several of our members decided to return to their earlier faith traditions, armed with the experience of a caring community and their re-connection to God. We had now become the "Church of the Revolving Door"!

An unspoken but clearly understood message now defined our lives and our mission: "Come and spend some life with us; reconnect to your spirit and God's Spirit. Open your spiritual eyes to the presence of God in your life and then take this experience with you wherever you go." Most returned to their former religious life, including one orthodox Jew who returned to his orthodox beginnings. For others, it meant joining another faith community or exploring new creative expressions of Spirit in the world. For example, one of our members went overseas to become a part of the Findhorn Spiritual Community in Scotland.

While we never actively sought to enlarge our community, we also never asked people to remain when they were ready to leave. Although that may sound pretty normal in the life of the Church, it was the Spirit that drove this revolving door. People came to us looking for some kind of spiritual connection. When that connection was made, they took their renewed spirit back into the world where it could have a new expression and mission.

Embedded in The New Church were a core of people who sustained the community by their continuing presence and devotion. Because they were alive, well and faithful, others could feel free to come and to leave, knowing that The New Church would continue without them. In a conventional church, which is playing the numbers game, this kind of freedom to come and go would be intolerable in terms of budgets and goals. For us, it was a gift. In The New Church, we were all enabled by the Spirit to welcome and also to let go. It was one of our greatest pleasures to serve this function for God.

The New Church was becoming a universal home. The barriers of other traditions were left outside, like shoes on a doormat, so that we could gather at our interfaith "water hole" and be God's family, gathered in worship and love. Each worship service was appropriately unique in its substance and message because we were a fluid community engaged in a constantly changing life that required God's presence and Spirit for our survival.

Lessons and Gifts of The New Church

While looking at ways to address the challenges of a changing world, we discovered new forms of ministry and worship. First, we discovered a mission to engage a diverse community in moment-by-moment experiences with the presence of God.

Second, by sharing the function of ministry, we removed the barriers between clergy and congregation, humanizing each, and discovering a new concept of ministry as a common devotion of all people to the Glory of God.

Third, those who entered our community as "unchurched" or "burned" by their former church connection found a new kind of church experience and a new home, in which they could practice acts of devotion and could flourish in an atmosphere of open-ness to individual and collective spiritual needs.

Fourth, although we never sought to include people from other religious traditions, we were enriched by those who found us and remained a part of our community. The freedom to worship together, without losing our individual traditions, introduced us to infinite possibilities for healing and reconciliation between us.

A final, critical gift in The New Church was the experience of "Spiritual Intimacy," the felt presence of God in our lives. Whether alone with God or in a community of others, people learned to recognize and talk about the presence of God in their lives and were encouraged to take that conversation into the world. Spiritual Intimacy allows us to see each other as gifts from God to be honored and celebrated. In talking about life and God, we discovered that our community of equals was deeply enhanced because it was also a community of differences. We were becoming one, as is our God.

Connections Between the Church in the Gym and The New Church

The Church in the Gym allowed us to see what happens in a church setting when an ordinary group of people gather to acknowledge God's presence and to connect with the reality of God in each moment of our lives. With the emergence of The New Church, our interfaith component created a more universal form of community in which powerful differences created connections, rather than divisions. We could visibly see and experience the oneness we shared as people while we discovered the oneness we shared in our religious and creedal lives.

In both "the church within a church" (A Church in a Gym) and a church completely outside of institutional structures (The New Church), we discovered our mutual hunger for spiritual connections. In the midst of our diversity, we experienced our common need to be connected to God and to each other. We recognized once more our profound need for community.

A Church in the Gym was a constant in a changing world. The threat of disturbing historical changes was modified and understood within the larger context of the constancy of God present in all of life. The New Church became an anchor in a complex world where our differences actually offered us an opportunity to discover an unexpected unity as the people of God.

Putting these two models together gave us a picture of a Church for the twenty-first century, a church that had to exist and thrive in a world which would continue to change while also being grounded in the constancy of the presence of God in each moment. We found a model for sustaining a vital common life in a world of difference and diversity by focusing on our shared and mutual need for connection, both spiritual and relational.

Yet Another God Surprise?

As we reflected on our experience in the New Church, we began to realize that the lessons we had learned are directly transferable to any existing church situation. These lessons can be summarized as:

1. Expanding the spiritual ministry and involvement of the community is a powerful way to energize the church.
2. Creating closer connections between community and pastor through experiences of shared ministry works directly to re-energize the clergy and to prevent the growing problem of clergy burnout.
3. Looking at creative opportunities for worship brings new spirit into old and familiar ways of being a worshiping community.
4. Examining economic issues in the church with new strategies to include more community participation and less clergy time might significantly reduce some of the costs of maintaining a church.
5. Introducing the concept of "caring and devotion" creates a direct antidote to struggles of power and control.
6. Becoming a community that values differences and celebrates diversity opens the door to more interfaith and inclusive opportunities to expand our connections with others in our community and in the world.
7. Reaffirming the need for the Church to live and grow in the world as a Spiritual force helps us to see the challenges of change in the larger picture of transformation and opportunity.

As we came to understand the lessons learned in the New Church, predictably and right on time, God re-entered the picture to surprise us with a new opportunity to look at the presence of God on an even larger stage. This time, we were led back into established religious communities, but now, armed with all we had learned from our New Church mission outside of the Church. We would return, not just to one church, but to over 150 congregations, Catholic, Protestant, and Reform Jewish, to see more of God's generosity in action.

Our new "numbers" (now a gift!) would help us validate what we had come to understand: diversity has the potential to create indelible and powerful spiritual connections.

God was about to become very Real to over three thousand people!

PART FOUR

A CHURCH BEYOND THE CHURCHES: GATHERING STORIES, BUILDING BRIDGES

CHAPTER 9

THE SPIRITUAL HEALING PROJECT: OPENING A BRAND NEW DOOR

God never stands still for long. In the middle of life in The New Church, the further adventures of the surprises of God began inauspiciously—an innocent question that seemed to appear out of nowhere. I wondered out loud one day, "Do you suppose others have had a similar experience of the presence of God that healed my spirit and transformed my life?" The unspoken response was clearly "yes!" Probably millions of people have experienced the transforming presence of God. The next question arrived immediately: "How could I find them to hear their stories?" The answer to that question would take us into the lives of literally thousands of people in diverse religious communities all over the United States. For the next ten years, my husband and I would be simultaneously engaged in our familiar New Church experience and a new research project which grew beyond our wildest fantasies!

Our research helped us to find God, literally, everywhere—weaving in and out of our consciousness like a new spirit of knowing, drenching us in the love and Spirit of God. It would change us in ways we couldn't even imagine, let alone plan.

The Project

This latest God Surprise had its own name, filled with the same boldness, excitement and audacity of The New Church. We called it "The Spiritual Healing Project," or, simply, "the project." Initially, the "project" was a modest research study to answer the question: Did other people have experiences similar to mine with the Presence of God in their life and how would they describe them? Using the words, "spiritual healing" as our descriptive language, we chose two questions to provide our answer:

1. What do the words "spiritual healing" mean to you? What words do you associate with this phrase?
2. What stories do you tell of "spiritual healing," according to your definition, in order to understand those words in a personal life setting?

We focused our study entirely on the meaning of the words, "spiritual healing" in order not to become engaged in discussions about the nature of God or other intellectual debates about theology or other church-related topics. Though carrying some negative connotations, the words "spiritual healing" also provided a generic umbrella under which people could discover their own answers to the questions being raised. Our first question was meant to enable us to build a spiritual vocabulary; the second, to create an archive of testimony to God's surprising activity in the world.

Our initial, modest plan called for my husband and I to visit fifteen or twenty UCC churches in our region and, at each, to listen to anyone who wanted to talk about spiritual healing. As researchers, our job was to listen and learn, not to offer information or opinions. People would also be asked to complete a nine-page questionnaire designed specifically to provide additional data for this study. We would also collect these questionnaires at the end of each meeting, thereby insuring that we would actually have some questionnaires to process.

Presenting our plan to the denomination for approval and endorsement introduced an alternative possibility we'd never considered. In a benignly-intended response to our plan, they said: "No one is interested in the subject of spiritual healing in the United Church of Christ. So why would you want to do that sort of thing? It doesn't make any sense." Baffled by their response, I found myself assuring them we weren't asking for any money to do the project. We had already moved from a question to a commitment. Fifteen or twenty churches in the Chicago area would be manageable. But not doing the study was not an option. Under these new conditions, our project proposal was accepted, but with renewed caution.

Invite a large number of churches to participate in the study in the hopes that a few would say "yes" was the advice. Not very encouraging. There was some doubt even that would happen. But God's plan turned out to be anything but modest!

The Sample

Undaunted by denominational disbelief, and with God's help and some special people to assist us, we picked out an amazing sample of one hundred churches in the United Church of Christ (UCC) located across the United States that reflected the rich diversities of the denomination: ethnic, socioeconomic, geographic; large/small; suburban/urban/rural; growing/not growing; multi-staff/single pastor; female pastors/male pastors, open and affirming/not open and affirming; etc. We even discovered and invited a multi-denominational community sharing the same facility to participate.

We, then, wrote to our one hundred churches asking if they would let two strangers into their community to ask two questions about "Spiritual Healing" in a group setting where everyone was welcome and no one had to say anything. To our absolute surprise, in two weeks, we had received replies from ninety-six congregations who all said "yes," welcoming our Spiritual Healing Project like an old friend coming to visit. Four more congregations asked to participate, creating a sample of one hundred churches that ranged in location from Bucks County, Pennsylvania to Watts in Los Angeles; from Portland, Oregon to Miami, Florida; from Texas to Maine; and all points in between.

Dazzled by God's generous Spirit, we paused to try to comprehend the breadth of the study we were about to undertake and "remembered" that we had expansively stated we would pay for the entire project ourselves rather than ask for financial support. We could rationalize this unusual decision on the basis that it would result in a non-biased (as much as is possible) study without influence from limits imposed by, or the prejudicial interests of, a funding agency. By paying for everything ourselves, we would also be assured that the project would actually take place and not be bogged down in some bureaucratic procedure that might take months to complete. However, we also now had a sample ten times what we had originally anticipated. We looked at each other, hesitating only for the briefest fraction of time, and then pronounced the word that would guide our work for the next fourteen years: an unequivocal, unqualified, unrestricted "Yes!"

If this is the gift that God has given us, this is what we will do. We signed on for the duration, whatever that would turn out to be and turned the whole thing over to God.

Phase 1: The Protestant (or, UCC) Study

To understand the Spiritual Healing Project, one needs to hear the "story" of its unfolding, a story of God's Actions in the world. Unlike other research endeavors with hypotheses to prove or disprove and reviews of the current literature to provide an existing context, the Spiritual Healing Project simply grew as a gift from God. As with all God Gifts, the locus of control remained under God's jurisdiction and not ours. We were simply God's agents, taking each moment as a precious gift to be honored and followed. We found ourselves on a true journey of trust and connection, without asking for reasons or directions.

As with all good stories, it begins with a customary formula to set the stage for all that is to come. One cannot begin the story until they are spoken. And so...

Once upon a time, we packed our bags and headed on the road to meet with members of our first congregation, an African American church in Chicago. The year was 1996. The month was April. Our hearts were filled with the presence of God and the excited openness of not knowing what we would find. We held our breath and entered the church.

About thirty people were waiting for us, seated in a room with a marvelous array of food and refreshment and warmly welcomed us. Expecting nothing, we discovered God present in each word and story shared. Enriched and humbled by our experience, we headed for St. Louis and our second church.

Exactly two years later, in April 1998, we visited our 100th church on a Native American Indian Reservation in South Dakota. There were no slot machines or any variety of gambling devices available. There were no gambling profits either. The church had a dirt floor and housed a small congregation that had suffered from years of missionary attempts to convert them to the right way of being Christian. Here, too, in this small congregation, we heard stories of God's transforming presence in their lives. In their pain and very real suffering, they had not lost the Spirit of God in their community.

In those two years, between 1996 and 1998, we had been welcomed by over two thousand people, collected close to one thousand stories, and were profoundly changed ourselves. One cannot meet that number of people from all walks of life and social backgrounds across the United States without being deeply affected by the wonder and mystery of human life as it intersects with the Divine Presence. We had met people of all backgrounds and abilities, but they all had something in common—they all had been equally touched by the experienced presence of God. They felt transformed by the loving actions of God; they described themselves as God's children living in God's surprising presence. Some were healed of their disease while others were not healed of the disease—but all of them were healed in spirit..

The entire experience became particularly moving in the light of the prediction that "no one in the UCC" would be interested in our study. By telling us how few people would be interested, we extended our study well beyond anything we would have ever planned, much less imagined. What an amazing gift and unexpected opportunity: clearly another God Surprise.

Gramma's Crazy Mission

In keeping with our new mission, and with no prompting, our grandchildren came up with their version of what we were doing. They called the project, "Gramma's Crazy Mission," a description that was entirely accurate. Like most children, they saw the truth and spoke it. It was crazy—and wonderful and unbelievably real and filled with the surprises and presence of God.

Since we conducted our research with almost no expectations of what we might find, each word, each story became an unexpected gift of God's abundance. What we saw was God's unlimited and powerful presence in ordinary moments of life; God Surprises transforming people everywhere. What we really found was a "Church in the Gym" in the heart of every church we visited.

Phase 2: Roman Catholics

After we completed the survey among UCC Churches, we congratulated ourselves on the accomplishment of our work and allowed ourselves a few moments of gratitude and satisfaction for a job well done. We even started to think about writing a book to document this Gift we had received. But God had other plans for us. No sooner had we finished our Protestant study, then the next surprise arrived as the first in a new series of questions, starting with: "What about the Catholic Church? Shouldn't it be included?" The thought had never crossed our minds.

Through a friend, we found a Catholic woman who matched the ethnic and socio-economic diversity in our UCC sample with a sample of parishes in the Archdiocese of Chicago. The unmistakable imprint of God! Ask and you shall receive more than you ever dreamed possible, placed directly at your front door.

We found a welcoming home in these Catholic communities, spending the year between 1998 and 1999 collecting Catholic words and stories. In each church, we always ended our presentation with the words, "Thank you for letting a couple of Protestants into your community to ask you about spiritual healing." Once a man responded, "I've been with you for over two hours and I don't see any Protestants!" We understood completely. We hadn't seen any Catholics either.

When our Catholic sample was complete, we had the same familiar fantasy of being finished. But God, the abundant provider, had yet another question for us: "What about the Jewish Community? It would be a mistake to leave them out." We agreed, not having any idea how we could accomplish this task.

Phase 3: Reform Jews

In one of those moments when we are suddenly confronted with the Mystery of God's Presence in this world, I "remembered" that nearly thirty years prior to our spiritual healing project, I had written my doctoral dissertation using an original questionnaire with a sample of Catholic, Protestant and Reform Jewish women in my research. Was it be possible that the same Rabbi who helped me thirty years earlier might still be alive or even at the same Temple where I conducted my research? Surely not. But surely God!

The same Rabbi was at the same Temple, two months from retirement. I phoned, assuming he wouldn't remember the graduate student who asked for his help so many years prior. He responded, "I do. What do you want this time?" I wanted, and gratefully received, his help as an entry point into the Reform Jewish community in Chicago, mid-Illinois and southern Wisconsin. We spent the year between 1999 and 2000 listening to words and stories in Jewish Reform synagogues.

Once again we were welcomed and profoundly moved by the openness of our Jewish participants. As a man put it succinctly at the end of one of our meetings: "You mean . . . we could talk this way with each other?" And we responded with a resounding and heart-felt "YES"!

Phase 4: Episcopalians

At the same time, an innocent inquiry arrived from a friend asking why we were discriminating against the Episcopal Church since I was a baptized Episcopalian—which I am. We knew the "real source" of that question and complied immediately. The Episcopal Bishop of Chicago welcomed us, and our project, and we alternated between Reform Jewish and Episcopal congregations while our supply of words and stories about God increased, growing like wild flowers in an open field in the Spring.

There was a wonderful familiarity in the words and stories of those with whom we spoke in the Episcopal and Reform Jewish congregations, which matched our experiences in the United Church of Christ and the Catholic Church. We were welcomed, not as strangers, but as fellow travelers on a road of discovery, receivers of the wonder of God captured in everyday moments in ordinary life. Different in mind, body, life circumstances and creed, but not in Spirit, we spoke a universal language that bound us to each other.

We had become the people of God.

Phases 5: Around the World

Two more surprises arrived to expand our study beyond the continental U.S. and into the experience of those outside of Judaism and Christianity. First, an invitation to meet with military chaplains arrived. We talked with several groups of interfaith clergy serving in the Army and Navy around the world, including representatives from the Muslim community.

Second and finally, we received a remarkable opportunity to visit Oxford University in England and present our work to the Alistar Hardy Religious Experience Research Centre, a worldwide organization that collects stories of spiritual healing from all the major religious traditions. As we brought our stories from the Spiritual Healing Project to this wonderful centre of interfaith studies, they gifted us with more stories from Judeo-Christian, as well as non-Judeo-Christian, sources. We opened the door into the reality of God present in the whole world. Carefully housed in an archival center, we read hundreds of stories about spiritual healing from most of the world religions. These stories contained at least thirty themes that were amazingly similar to the themes in our stories. We now understood that we were looking at a phenomenon that carried worldwide implications and already contained the seeds of a universal language of healing.

The Universality of God

As we continued to experience the interfaith diversity of our New Church, God was opening our eyes to a much larger reality. What might have been a localized phenomenon was now clearly shared across the globe and among many religious traditions. We were privileged to observe a worldwide screen of transformation and connection. God was real, unlimited by any people-made distinctions and beyond every descriptive statement we could make.

Our small, manageable study had grown to include nearly three thousand people who shared their stories of God present in their lives wherever we went. Ordinary words were becoming limited and nearly useless containers for the profound nature of our experience. Instead, we were filled with a growing and breathtaking sense of Mystery and Awe.

We dared to wonder what might happen if one approached life and death hostilities between religious traditions from the point of our common experiences of the presence and action of God. Ordinarily our differences set us against each other. But could the powerful commonalities we were finding in our unexpected interfaith study give us a new starting point for the process of healing? Could our differences be honored within the larger monotheistic context we shared and offer a new language of healing to contain our animosities?

We waited to discover where God would lead us next.

CHAPTER 10

WHEN GOD BECOMES REAL TO MANY:
A STORY OF CONNECTION

W hen we finally stopped long enough to write our first book about the project, *Healing the Spirit: Stories of Transformation*,[6] we felt deeply moved
both by the simplicity of the project and the profound implications of our findings.
One simple question had been transformed into a life mission among an unfolding
company of people located throughout the United States and in England. One could
scarcely keep up with the gifts we were collecting.

Yet we still had one undeveloped resource that could take us to a new level of
understanding in terms of our study. We had two thousand, nine-page questionnaires
sitting in my closet waiting to be data processed and analyzed. Their secrets remained
hidden because we couldn't afford the statistical analysis necessary to unpack them.
Receiving an estimate of $50,000, we had hit our first brick wall! Until . . . another
God Surprise. We should have known that God wasn't about to let this opportunity
slip away.

The Riches of the Questionnaires Revealed

My son is a research psychologist at the University of Pennsylvania. Through his efforts, we identified a group at Johns Hopkins Medical Center in Baltimore who could
data process our questionnaires at a price we could afford. After visiting with the
group we celebrated the glorious generosity of God and this marvelous opportunity
to complete our work and sent our questionnaires to Baltimore immediately.

Within three months we had powerful data for everything that had been shared
in our group experiences. Words, stories, and detailed descriptions of the spiritual
healing experience and its history along with demographics to describe our participants brought the project to life with new specificity and vividness. We felt a powerful
wave of surprise and gratitude. Each story was now reinforced by a written "picture"
of the person who had shared it, allowing others to learn more about God directly
from another person. In our imagination, we hoped people would say, "If God can
happen to them, God can happen to me!" We now had decisive and documented
evidence that God was real and available to people everywhere, as close as the next
moment and as intimately possible as their next heart beat. We had been entrusted

with a Truth that transcended anything we had known or lived prior to the project and were more than ever determined to give that gift to as many who would receive it.

What Did We Learn?

From people of all backgrounds and traditions, we learned a universal definition of the meaning and experience of Spiritual Healing. As if in one voice they said, "Spiritual Healing is an experience of the presence or action of God in my life which has transformed me." By transformed, they meant, God had become "real" to them. God happened anywhere, everywhere, but, most particularly, when two or three gathered to talk about God. People told us that God didn't necessarily make their lives "better" but they became infinitely "richer" than they could ever have imagined or planned.

God's Presence is a Healing Experience

Spiritual healing is a process of connection between God and God's people. Regardless of socio-economic status, geographic location, ethnic background, color, gender, sexual preference or creed—knowing and experiencing God's presence is a universal solvent, which changes people's self identity and transforms their lives.

No form of magic words or interventions can produce a Spiritual Healing nor can any number of steps or strategies create God's presence. God is God, fully in charge, and one needs only to acknowledge God's presence to discover the possibilities inherent in God's transforming reality.

God became "real" for the people in our study. They did not equivocate nor minimize the experience in any way. They spoke to us of God's presence in their lives and did not hesitate to use "God language" to describe their experience.

But they also told us that they didn't talk about such things to others for fear of being seen as weird, crazy or too religious, and rarely shared their experiences in Church or Synagogue settings.

For many, this was the first time they had ever shared their stories.

There are Three Kinds of Spiritual Healing

Three kinds of healing experiences occurred: (1) a physical healing in the presence of a disease, the so-called "miracle" cures; (2) a healing in which a disease is not cured but where people experienced a healing of the spirit, individually or collectively; and, (3) healings which occur in the ordinary flux of life, with or without a disease or stressor.

In our sample, the most frequently described form of spiritual healing were of this third type, a healing experience in the midst of life, spontaneously occurring. These experiences occur everywhere and anywhere people become aware of the surprising presence of God in their immediate circumstances.

Healing has a Before and an After

What preceded these experiences of God's Presence and the actual experience itself were described in a variety of remarkably similar stories which included themes of surrender, the letting go of control, acceptance, surprise, transformation, the experience of "peace," and being physically, emotionally and spiritually healed. These experiences generally happened—but not always—without prayer, preparation, a crisis, or a longing for change. They happened as an unexpected surprises in the midst of life that pointed toward a new direction with God at the center.

After experiencing God's healing presence, people reported feeling loved by God; feeling closer to one's neighbors and family; living more in the moment; being less angry; wanting to do more for others; looking for actions to reflect the gift that had been given; and, wanting to return to one's religious community with more spirit and energy.

Healing Transforms Self-Identity, Life-Patterns and Action-Orientation

In their stories of healing, we found a powerful commonality and connection between very diverse groups of people. While they might be different on the outside, they were deeply connected internally through their common experiences of God in their lives. The same theme prevailed throughout the study: God was present, real and active in ordinary life, and available to all people. Creedal differences simply disappeared in the content of the stories. You could have tossed them on a table and not been able to pick out the Reform Jewish from the Protestant and Catholic stories, unless certain distinctive terms, such as "Rabbi" appeared.

People spoke of changes in their self-identity, the way they saw themselves after their spiritual healing. These included feeling: more like a child of God; more a part of God's creation; stronger and more compassionate; less judgmental; calmer; and, more centered and self-accepting.

They also spoke of changes in their patterns of living. As examples, after their healing, respondents reported being: less angry; more open to God and God's direction in my life; more open to their "neighbor"; more anxious to be of service; more constant in devotional, prayer and worship life; and, living more "in the moment," which meant they had a stronger sense of acting in the "now" rather than in the past or future.

Finally, people spoke of becoming more action-oriented, of feeling the need to take more initiative to participate in the world following the experience when God became Real. People wanted to be able to "do" something, which would reflect the gift they had been given. Often they expressed the wish to become more active in their religious community.

Healing Stories are Contagious

To our amazement, we discovered that by the simple sharing of stories of God present and active in a group setting, the group itself became infused with God's Presence and was transformed. Healing stories are contagious! Hearing a story from another can also awaken my own story or provide me with a framework for something I had experienced but didn't know how to name. When someone I respect or trust shares their experience, it also affirms and validates my own.

Healing Invites Recovering Awareness

Repeatedly we learned that God is a gift, offered to all who will recognize and receive it. Simply receiving a gift may sound easy. However, in the complicated text of our lives and until we are released from our cultivated "unawareness," we are unable to appreciate the presence of God in the constancy that it is offered. Before we began our mission, we were similarly unaware of God's ubiquitous presence. Nothing prepared us for the magnitude of what we would find. Yet, knowing nothing, we were open to learning everything. Expecting nothing allowed our spirits to be filled with the abundance of God. Allowing ourselves to be a blank screen allowed God to create a Technicolor production, exceeding anything Hollywood could produce.

Another Surprise: George Gallup and Book #2

In a wonderfully serendipitous way, we met George Gallup, Jr., through a woman from the Christian Science Church who attended a workshop we were giving for the International Association of Parish Nurses in St. Louis. Only God could organize such a scenario.

We shared our data just processed at Johns Hopkins with him. We told him the story of our mission and what we had learned in our face-to-face meetings with the people in our study. He carefully examined our data, read our book, and pronounced our work as worthy to speak for the nation: "a clear and lively portrait of the baseline dimensions of spirituality of the U.S. Population."[7] Affirming the importance of our work, he continues: "It is exciting to reflect upon the potential that this imposing body of qualitative and quantitative research has for bringing about healing relationships among people at the deepest level. The authors have done the scientific and religious worlds a great service in probing beneath the surface of life to give us new and fresh insight into the action and presence of God in human existence."[8]

He became a friend. Another gift from God.

At his suggestion, we wrote a second book, *Taking a Chance on God: Exploring God's Presence in our Lives*, to include a whole new set of stories and information from the data we had just processed and analyzed.[9] He even agreed to provide a foreword and actually suggested the title!

Three Unexpected Issues Arise

In the midst of our passion and joy, several issues emerged to remind us of other realities in life. Collecting stories of healing was not enough. We also had to help people find or create places to tell their stories. While God was Real in our study, so is the world's resistance to that truth.

The first issue had to do with safety of expression. Where can you openly and safely talk about the experience of God in your life? Anywhere? Everywhere? To anyone? Well, not really. Even though the people in our study readily shared their stories in our group data gathering session, these same people reported that they rarely shared these life-changing experiences with anyone. Not with their family, spouse or significant other. Certainly, not in their religious community. The reasons given were simple: talking about the presence of God in their lives could be construed by some as weird, crazy or too religiously conservative—attributions no one wanted. My own experience affirmed the reality of these painful responses. But the result of such choices automatically deprives other people of the powerful spiritual energy that is released when people share their experiences with others. The opportunity to help others identify the presence of God in their lives is lost under a blanket of distrust and deep fears of judgment. Everyone loses.

The second problem was quite surprising and unexpected. For many clergy, talking about their own spiritual lives was considered inappropriate, especially in a group setting. It was far easier to speak of the spiritual life of a member of their congregation than to share their own experiences with God. One clergy woman put it to me bluntly: "You know, we're tough and we're just private and independent people. Don't expect us to reveal anything about ourselves. We just won't do it!" Is there something within current understandings of ministry that forces clergy to be personally anonymous where God is concerned? Yet, it was more than that. In a world that is spiritually fractured, all of us are individually and collectively responsible to invite people to learn of the presence of God in our lives so that others may discover God's presence in their lives as well. That is the obligation of the gift we have been given. In fact, when clergy withhold their own stories, the entire congregation is deprived of the life-changing possibilities of seeing God in their lives. An unconscious message is passed on to the congregation that personal experiences are not appropriate in our religious services. It's a message we cannot afford to be sending.

Finally, it also became clear that not everyone wanted to know about the gift we treasured. Was the promise of change that the Spirit carries too much of a burden in an already over-burdened world? Is the state of "unawareness" more overwhelming than we realize? Does indifference join with fear to create an impenetrable wall that keeps people from seeing God's gifts in their lives?

These realities were clear indicators that defensive resistance was even more profound than we realized in some arenas, making the revelations of our study all the more essential both to the church and to the world.

Three Thousand People and Still Growing

While resistance may exist, it is also true that, at this point, three thousand people have now participated in our studies and programs. Our books and other resources provide additional avenues to proclaim the message we've experienced. Gifts from God must be given away. The miracle is that they always grow in us exponentially as we give them away to others.

In the fourteen years since the spiritual healing project began we have moved from a simple question to an astounding array of experiences of God's Presence everywhere. There are no adequate words to describe how powerfully this journey has transformed our lives.

In addition, it appears that God is far from finished with us. For instance, when we looked more closely at the data we had collected, we discovered the potential for two new studies within the responses to the questionnaire. The first we called an inquiry into Spiritual Life in the Aging Process. Its central question is: Does one's spiritual life change after age 60? The second is titled: The Meaning of Spiritual Health, and concerns questions, such as: What constitutes a state of "spiritual health? Can spiritual health stand on its own, separate from the physical or emotional components of being human?

Once again, we were on the road to learn what God had to teach us about spiritual life in old age. With both a sacred and secular sample and a new questionnaire, our lives were opening to a new look at God's Presence in the process of aging and a beginning look at the meaning of spiritual health. We became researchers once again.

In addition, with the wealth of information we had accumulated and the advent of our new studies, we sensed a need for a more permanent "home" and connection for our data and other voices to proclaim the generous love and presence of God. Enter the Chicago Theological Seminary (CTS), home for not only UCC students preparing for ministry, but also a teaching institution where a rare ethnic, socio-economic, geographic, preference and creedal diversity of people are preparing to bring God's word into the world: Exactly the right environment for our interfaith project!

Part of our data is now housed as an archive in CTS' Hammond Library. We also became adjunct faculty, developing and teaching two courses for seminary students. We had found a new venue for our project and new voices to carry our message. The wonder and gift of this opportunity is surely mind-boggling! Assuming that each seminary student encounters a thousand people in her or his years of ministry, and given the numbers of seminarians in our first two classes, we had already reached a potential of 21,000 people who would have access to the materials we had presented to our students. Each additional class we might teach contains the same potential. Another God Surprise! Another gift.

Conclusion

Reflecting on the breadth of our project, I find myself, unsurprisingly, in a constant state of awe and gratitude for everything that had preceded it. Our vision in the Church in the Gym had been to rename the church as that place where people gather to speak about God and to recognize God's constancy in a changing world. Our mission in the New Church was directed to the Church itself engaged in its own process of profound change. In the completion of that mission, we had found an entirely unexpected connection with the interfaith and under-churched populations. In fact, we had accomplished both our vision and mission through the outreach of "The Spiritual Healing Project." God was present in the lives of people everywhere, transforming people of all backgrounds and creeds into a three-thousand member community connected and focused on the constancy and reality of God Present in the world.

We also recognized that an unexpected cycle has become complete. We moved from within the church to outside the church and now back into the broad religious community to find the literally thousands of people who have experienced God in their lives. A new kind of "Mega-Community" has emerged from our latest journey: over 150 very diverse, interfaith congregations, united in their experiences of the presence and action of God in their lives. Their stories create a ongoing, ever-new picture of God, the great Surpriser, Initiator, Transformer and Mystery in the world, who also happens to be directly involved in each of our lives.

The universal possibilities for connections between different worlds of people within this amazing story are almost beyond description. They speak of the ubiquitous Presence of God in each of our lives, waiting to be acknowledged and released into the world. A universal celebration of common spiritual experiences becomes the catalyst for connection and healing.

Praise God! Praise God!

CHAPTER 11

A CHURCH FOR TODAY: THE MULTIFACETED PEOPLE OF GOD

Our journey has taken us through sixty years of history and a vast array of powerful changes in the church and in society. As all changes involve both a letting go of the "old" and an opening of the "new," they also present us with lessons to be learned and gifts to be received. Not infrequently, we are not aware of the gifts until some later date when they suddenly shift our attention into a new direction. "Oh, that was what that was all about" or "It didn't make sense before" or, simply, "Now I get it."

These lessons remind us that we operate in a circular continuum as we grow through life, rather than a two-dimensional model of forward or backward. In fact, we go through life living in a series of contiguous circles, something like a gyroscope, in which the circles rotate around each other while moving steadily within some kind of larger, undefined God Space and God Time. There are beginnings, middles and endings, intermingled with circles of birth, life and death. There is a circle from the body to the heart to the spirit and another from my being to your being and to our life together. Each is a pathway of connection. In spiritual terms, we move from God, into the world, and back to God again.

Following each circle we find ourselves arriving in a new space while also returning to our original place, enlightened and enriched by what we have experienced and learned. So each ending opens the door to a new beginning and each death carries with it the promise and surprise of a new life. This book is, as well, the story of a journey from within the church or religious community to the outside world and back into the place from which it began.

Finding the Heart and Spirit of the Church

The Church in the Gym was the "heart of the church," as it embodied both the presence of God and the heart/spirit of those who allowed God's presence to transform their lives within a larger community. It also operated as a present day symbol of the unexpected nature and surprising circumstances of God's presence. Being in a gym was as unlikely a home for the living Christ as was the manger. It simply is not the sort of place where one ordinarily looks for God. The sanctuary, the Chapel, and, perhaps, the library were more likely places. Even the Sunday school rooms had a stated and recognizable God agenda in them. But the gym . . . well hardly.

Yet, unmistakably, God and the heart and spirit of the community were here, on the bare floors, under the basketball hoops, within the high ceilings and windows, located in an area of folding chairs, a small, unadorned podium—and filled with people.

The heart of the community comes to life when the Spirit of God's presence connects to the spirits and lives of those present. It's as simple as that. When we acknowledge God's Presence, God IS present, whoever and wherever we are.

Becoming a Community of Spirit

When the Church in the Gym moved out into the world in the form of The New Church, the freedoms we had experienced entered the non-traditional world of a "church outside of the Church." We were now a nomadic people without a regular church home (as in a building we claimed and maintained) but with the spirit and energy of the Presence of God leading us through a kind of secular wilderness of questions: Where shall we be? How shall we express ourselves as a church? Who will walk with us on this unchartered path? How do we minister to the Church?

What we found were people from other faith communities who were also seeking a new relationship with God and a different kind of spiritual experience. What we learned was how much we had in common. In the midst of our corporate life, we experienced an interfaith environment in which our diversity became our special gift. We became a body of believers and questioners, people of all ages and backgrounds, bound together by a common language of God's creative abundance. Our community offered a place to learn about God; a way station for travelers who need rest and refreshment for the journey and a launching pad for their mission into life.

Discovering God's Abundant Healing Activity throughout the World

When we returned to more established religious communities (150 Christian and non-Christian communities of faith) in the Spiritual Healing Project, we found 3,000 people sharing a common and transforming experience of the presence of God in their lives. God was real and new lives were everywhere!

Never imagining we would find a universal definition of spiritual healing which would transcend the barriers and boundaries of diversity, we were presented with one definition of the transforming presence of God and a common language of healing that seemingly speaks to everyone—whether Reform Jew, Catholic or Protestant, Military Chaplain or Research Fellow.

Never dreaming we would find similar kinds of stories in an interfaith sample, we were gifted with hundreds of stories from Protestant, Catholic and Reform Jewish congregations that speak in one voice of the presence of God in their lives.

We have hoped that one day we might include the voice of Islam in our study and discover Muslim congregations who would be willing to become a part of our research. It would enable us to reach out to all who speak of the "One God" we share and the possibility that our words and stories, spoken together, might enable us to look at our spiritual connections rather than our radical differences.

Hearing each other speak about God in our lives helps us to discover an undeniable commonality of experience. As this first step is taken, the path toward a new vision of the Multifaceted People of God becomes possible. Starting with our differences seldom reaches the place of our mutual understanding.

Avoiding Despair and Disillusion

Looking at mainstream religious congregations today in terms of statistics alone creates a deep sense of despair. Many of the mainstream churches in the U.S. are steadily losing members. Some denominations seem engaged in a kind of dying process, even as a number of large, successful congregations from a variety of traditions continue to grow.

When faced with the reality of dying or death, we feel an immediate regret and sadness. Most often, we respond by increasing our efforts to find a "cure" or move headlong into the future, initiating something to divert our attention. But such responses cost us the "gift" that resides in every human process that is allowed to move through death into new life. In fact, we cannot observe God's actions in a process we choose to avoid.

The church reflects the culture in which we live and its growing state of disillusion. We who live with plenty find ourselves feeling increasingly empty. Our technological world traps us each day in an overload of choices. We turn, again and again, from glimpses of God's presence to the ache of our own illusions of abandonment. We ignore the signs of hope and focus on signs of gloom. Reading the newspaper headlines or watching the news on television could easily convince us that any hope for a peaceful future is a memory of the past. Yet, on the second or third page of the same paper, we read of miraculous medical breakthroughs and find stories of people who care and connect with others in loving and protective actions. As God's people, the church should be the first place to identify the possibilities that can emerge out of tragedy—yet too often we fail to do so. Too often, we try to solve our despairs and disillusions by retreating into our individual cocoons to wait and watch in resignation, rather than trusting these uncomfortable experiences of growth and change to be actually moving us into the future. In our Christian language, such responses mean that we linger in the experience of death, not proceeding through it to the gift of Resurrection.

In these last fourteen years, as we pursued the Spiritual Healing Project, we have lived and breathed on the other side of despair with people of hope and faithful trust. The people we have met live in the real world of disease and brokenness, but they have found God's presence and actions in the midst of that very same world. Rather than seeing the world and life as hopeless and out of control, they have found the gift of God's presence to be a transforming moment that introduces them to a new life with God in the heart of it. While they would acknowledge the reality that much of our world has gone "crazy" with anger and hate, they also are able to share stories of the presence of God in their lives. They have claimed God's faithful promise to be with each of us. They have experienced finding Grace where one would least expect to find it. For them, God has become real.

As one of our participants told us, "Now that I have AIDS and am blind, now I can finally see . . . and know what I have been in the past and where I am today. And now all the women are beautiful, and all the men are handsome, and I am so grateful for my disease . . . I have been healed."

Such stories challenge the church to rediscover its reason for existing, its purpose. The church must be that place where all people can openly express their experiences of the presence of God. Such stories, told and heard, are convincing evidence of the reality of God's presence in the world. God is real because people continue to experience God's presence and actions in the very center of ordinary life . . . right here, right now . . . in each moment of each day. God is real and available for all people everywhere. What extraordinary good news we have to tell!

The church now has the opportunity to renew and explore its identity as the Multifaceted People of God in the 21st century, joined together in our common experiences and language of God present to each of us. We are one people, grounded in God and connected through the gifts of our diversity. In sharing God's presence in each of our lives and recognizing the universality of that experience, we learn that God's Spirit is alive and well and functioning in this world according to the Mystery, Creation and Love of God.

We are not living as the abandoned children of God.

We dare not lose this moment nor be too afraid to let the Spirit lead us into the uncharted, unfamiliar, unknown and Infinite Presence of God. We have been given a common and universal language of experience.

Now we must learn to speak it.

CHAPTER 12

FINDING GOD AGAIN FOR YOURSELF: THE REQUIREMENT TO SHARE YOUR STORY

*I*n its beginnings, the church grew explosively because it attracted and welcomed so many different kinds of people into its ranks. It was truly the church of all the people, welcoming any who chose to join the community, regardless of age, status or gender. It also grew and thrived in times of great disruption, powerful resistance and deadly repercussions to those who became a part of the community. Today, given the amount of change we experience, our tendency is to provide more anchors and tighter structures to prevent our lives and institutions from collapsing. But the "spirit of change" calls us to look at a bigger picture, to ride out the storm, to reclaim the energy that is created by diversity, and to dare to speak openly about the ongoing presence of God, especially in times of challenge and disaster.

God is the God of the living, not the dead. The Community of the Multifaceted People of God, living as an expression of the Presence of God in the world today, is not dead either! Our mission calls for each of us to proclaim the Divine interaction between God and all of God's people as experienced at this time in history.

We have already seen the marvelous interplay between the constancy of God in the middle of ongoing change, and the diversity of people within the Oneness of God. As these two themes intersect and move through life, we can observe and become a part of the remarkable connection between change and diversity and the Creative Mystery we call God. We can trust the process of change, even when it is disorienting, because it is rooted in God's Constancy. We can honor all the diversity between us because it is held in the container of God's Oneness and Presence.

Too often, we struggle to keep our human systems in stasis, resisting that which seems inimical to our present state of being. But waiting on the other side of the fence that we straddle is the promise of new life, which God always brings to us. When we lose our connection to God's constant presence, we hang in the balance between the old and the new; the familiar and the unknown; the past and the future. When we reaffirm that God is Real and ready to surprise us, we can let go and be led into new possibilities.

Never more important than right now, those individuals and communities who acknowledge God's continuing presence must challenge the helplessness we feel in relation to these powerful changes of our recent history and bring us into the reality that God is not absent from our lives. It is only we who resist seeing God's presence in the middle of life as it unfolds around us. But we can look beyond our resistance. Transformation is always possible because God is always here. Seeing God in every moment means we can draw on God's immediate presence to transform that moment. Each moment can then unfold into the next, in a growing awareness of the reality of God in our life. The alternative is to position ourselves in the unyielding certainty of our helplessness and despair. We can see God in the newness of each breath we take or we can close our eyes, hold our breath and die.

How do You Begin?

Moving from despair to hope means choosing life over death. This seems an obvious choice. But how does one actually go about cultivating such awareness, such trust?

We have already established that there are no special programs or steps to create an experience of the Mystery of God's Presence. Instead, we have to rely on the ongoing presence and surprises of God to help us find our directions. We begin with our own heart and spirit to reconnect to those experiences in which God has become Real in our own lives.

The first thing to notice is that you are reading this book. This means that you are interested in, or at least curious about, beginning the process of rediscovering God. Having reached this final chapter, you have already exposed yourself to the Mystery of God that has been filling these pages with stories of God present and active in the world today. Your journey has begun.

To continue, beyond this book, you must simply begin to look at your own life to discover your story of the Presence or Action of God in your life. When did God become Real to you? When did you hear God's calling you into a new life? Where did God lead you? How is your life different now than it might have been without the Presence or Action of God in your life? Your memories constitute your first step.

Telling Your Story

As a further step beyond the state of recognition of God in your life, you need to share your experience of the Presence or Action of God with someone—anyone who will listen without judgment will do. Stories of God's presence in your own life can be wonderfully empowering. But they are not for you alone. Tucking them away in your heart is important but insufficient. Your stories need to go out to others so they may discover the presence of God in their lives. When you receive the gift of God's presence, you automatically become God's agent and messenger to others. In this new mission, there is an obligation to share your God story because it carries "life" into the world and creates a new spiritual connection between you and those who "hear" you with their spiritual eyes and hearts.

Enacting Your Story

The next stage in the process is to enact your story. Discovering and creating an Action Opportunity to bring your gift from God into the world as a visible landmark is a critical next step. What form that action will take is as varied as there are people. There are no rules, no regulations, to define your action. But you must take some action that will reflect your connection with the Mystery of God in your life. The freedom of God's Spirit to express itself through your actions is unlimited and always creative. However, it relies on you to extend your gift into the world. Without your action, God is without voice and movement.

Within these actions of claiming and telling your story and bringing your experience of God into the world in some active way, you will automatically discover more of God's presence because people will respond to your story with their stories. You will discover a new spiritual intimacy in your mutual sharing and listening. Such spiritual connections will transform your relationship with these others. Once you start looking in God's direction, your will find God growing exponentially and you will begin to see the constancy and Oneness of God expressed everywhere.

Each new voice spoken, each new story heard brings more people into the circle of God's presence.

From Your Story to New Models of the Church

Any place where people gather together to share their words and stories about God becomes infused with the presence of God. It may be an existing community that collects stories of God present and has chosen to provide a home for the spiritually "homeless." It may come to life among the voices of those who represent the heart of the church as they bring their experiences into the larger congregation. So, too, a group that gathers to speak of God's action in their lives but who have no established home may create a new setting for the Church. It could happen when churches combine their congregations and/or open their doors to all who want to learn about God, irrespective of their differences on the outside or the inside. It will come into being because God appears to be persistently and patiently seeking to bring us into connection and new life.

How all of this will actually come into being is part of the process of God's Creative Ministry of Surprises. But some of the pieces are already in place.

The Church is becoming more inclusive and looking at ways to decrease the divisions between us. Denominations are making contacts with other denominations to create a broader and deeper connection between them.

Some Churches are exploring ways to bring the non-ordained clergy into a more active place in the church and looking at other leadership possibilities for people called into religious vocations.

Interfaith dialogue is growing between Catholics, Protestants and Jews. We are extending invitations to others of different faith backgrounds to join with us in common worship and study experiences, as well as exploring mutual concerns within the social communities we share. Voices from the Muslim community are being invited to join into the dialogue and shared activity. The concept of the "Multifaceted People of God" is a powerful tool in acknowledging our common heritage while preserving our distinct spiritual identities. In fact, we become one spiritual community whenever we share our stories of God in our lives and discover that God, the Universal, Creative, Ultimate Mystery of Life is also right here in the moment with us. There is no dis-connect between us.

The challenge for us is to speak the words that describe the Presence of God in this time in history and trust in the process that is ignited by our words and actions. In other words, we are not trying to convert each other into one religious box. Rather, we are inviting each other to share in our various liturgies and to learn each other's God language in order to discover: the uniqueness of our traditions; the gifts of God we share in common; and the power that is contained in our connections to God and each other.

If we refuse to speak and fail to act, the Gift that God is offering will be negated and lost. The chaos, which is life lived without God at the center, will continue to overwhelm us. It is entirely our choice to re-discover the Holy One who loves us out of the darkness and into the light.

As a matter of fact, everything has been made ready and is in place:

God is here.
God is Real.
The moment is right now.
And yours is the final voice
that must be heard
to complete the connection.
Look for God in your heart.
Do not be afraid to speak.
New Life is waiting.
And so is God.

EPILOGUE:
WHEN GOD BECOMES REAL

The New Spiritual Community of the 21st century will be built on the *spirit* of the Baby Boomers, the *questions* of the Gen X'ers, and the *energy* of the Y2K Kids, as experienced in creative new models of faith and community.

The central activities of these communities will be to share experiences of God present and active in each person's life, to nourish both the individual and collective spirit and to encourage actions which will reflect God's presence in the world.

The unique character of these communities will be their inclusive nature in which each person is invited to reflect her or his own particular understanding of the reality and experience of God in the world. Diverse in age, cultural background, economic class and even religious affiliation, the members of this new spiritual community will be united in their common experiences of the presence of God in their lives while maintaining their religious differences.

What will this new spiritual community look like as it groans and stretches through its own delivery process? Like all new creations, it will bear evidence of the gifts of former times as it forges its way into a new form and structure. Its history will not be forgotten. Yet its shape will not be pre-determined by the past. Its form will be dynamic, alive, ever-changing and open to whatever the next God Surprise might be.

Whether occupying space in a building, meeting in a home or business, or gathering in cyber-space, its inclusive nature will rest on the foundation of each person's experience of God as real and active in his or her life. Sharing the stories of these experiences leads to an infinite variety of actions of devotion and service in the world and for the healing of the world.

Whether in groups of two or two thousand, worship becomes a moment by moment celebration of God's presence in our lives, not confined to specific times, days or spaces, but operating in response to God's generosity and presence in each moment of every day.

The New Spiritual Community will move from hierarchy to equality and mutuality; it will encourage the ministry and devotion of the entire community. It will explore the vision of God as "right here, right now," not "out there" in some unavailable space. It will see the recognition of God's Presence in our lives as the motivating force for actions taken for the transformation of the world.

The New Spiritual Community will reflect the immediacy and intimacy of experiences of God in which strength replaces power; choice replaces control; and devotion to the utter Mystery and Miracle of God emboldens our lives with the fullness and constancy of God's Presence.

WHEN GOD BECOMES REAL TO EACH ONE OF US...
THE WORLD WILL CHANGE.

Notes

1. George Gallup, Jr. and Timothy Jones, *The Next American Spirituality: Finding God in the 21st Century* (Colorado Springs: Victor Press, Cook Communications Ministries, 2000), 113.
2. Wendy Murray Zoba, "The Class of '00," *Christianity Today* (3 February 1997), 18; quoted in Gallup and Jones, *Next American Spirituality*, 117.
3. Gallup and Jones, *Next American Spirituality*, 117.
4. Carl S. Dudley and David A. Roozen, *Faith Communities Today: A Report on Religion in the United States Today* (Hartford, Connecticut: The Hartford Institute for Religion Research of Hartford Seminary, 2001), 11.
5. Dudley and Roozen, *Faith Communities Today*, 8.
6. Bobbie McKay and Lewis A. Musil, *Healing the Spirit: Stories of Transformation* (Allen, Texas: Thomas More Publications, 2000).
7. See George Gallup, Jr., "Foreword" in Bobbie McKay and Lewis A. Musil, *Taking a Chance on God: Exploring God's Presence in Our Lives* (iUniverse, 2007), v.
8. See George Gallup, Jr., "Foreword" in Bobbie McKay and Lewis A. Musil, *Taking a Chance on God: Exploring God's Presence in Our Lives* (iUniverse, 2007), vii.
9. See Bobbie McKay and Lewis A. Musil, *Taking a Chance on God: Exploring God's Presence in Our Lives* (iUniverse, 2007).

Made in the USA